The Relational Database
Dictionary

The Relational Database Dictionary

A comprehensive glossary of relational terms and concepts, with illustrative examples

C. J. Date

Beijing · Cambridge · Farnham · Köln · Paris · Sebastopol · Taipei · Tokyo

The Relational Database Dictionary
by C. J. Date

Published by O'Reilly Media, Inc., 1005 Gravenstein Highway North,
Sebastopol, CA 95472.

O'Reilly books may be purchased for educational, business, or sales
promotional use. Online editions are also available for most titles
(*safari.oreilly.com*). For more information, contact our corporate/
institutional sales department: (800) 998-9938 or *corporate@oreilly.com*.

Editor: Deborah Russell	**Cover Designer:** Karen Montgomery
Production Editor: Rachel Monaghan	**Interior Designer:** David Futato
Proofreader: Rachel Monaghan	**Illustrators:** Robert Romano and Jessamyn Read

Printing History:

August 2006:	First Edition.

ISBN-10: 0-596-52798-5
ISBN-13: 978-0-596-52798-3
[C]

Thy gift, thy tables, are within my brain
Full charactered with lasting memory,
Which shall above that idle rank remain
Beyond all date, even to eternity

—William Shakespeare, *Sonnet 122*

"When I use a word," Humpty Dumpty
said, in rather a scornful tone, "it means
just what I choose it to mean—neither
more nor less."

—Lewis Carroll, *Through the Looking-*
Glass and What Alice Found There

Lexicographer *A writer of dictionaries,*
a harmless drudge

—Dr. Johnson, *A Dictionary of the*
English Language

To all keepers of the true
relational flame

Foreword

The book you're holding is about words. Words enable us to communicate, but only when we share an understanding of what those words mean. In everyday life, the precise meaning of our words is often a bit fuzzy. You can tell me that you've "cut" yourself, and our shared understanding of what it means to be "cut" is good enough for most practical purposes. Show the doctor your cut, though, and she'll probably trot out the word "laceration" and charge you $60 for her trouble.

Indeed, in the field of medicine, the precise use of terminology is critical to proper care. Complain to your doctor of "dizziness," and you'll soon find her talking in terms of vertigo, disequilibrium, and pre-syncope. Why? Because "dizzy" is an ambiguous term. People apply the term "dizzy" to at least three distinct feelings, with different underlying causes that lead to differing treatments. The first step to diagnosing "dizziness" is to determine accurately and precisely what you are experiencing. Then, when talking about your treatment, your doctor will use very precise words that are carefully defined to eliminate ambiguity in communication between medical professionals.

Discussions about relational theory do not usually put your health at risk. However, they do lead to some very heated arguments. Terminology in our field is frequently co-opted by vendor marketing campaigns. Practitioners often adhere to fuzzy, imprecise, and sometimes just plain wrong definitions of terms. I've seen people argue in "violent agreement"—in full accord, but not realizing it—because they lacked a fully shared and precise definition of the words they were throwing at each other.

Our field is maturing. We are developing our own shared language. As in medicine, our language will enable us to communicate clearly and precisely about what we do. And again as in medicine, clarity and precision are critical to the success of our work, and ultimately to the success of our clients. Languages grow and change over time. C. J. Date's effort here is just the beginning. But it's a good beginning. To all who read this foreword and the book that follows, I wish you clarity—of thought, and in words.

—Jonathan Gennick
Munising, Michigan
June 2006

The Relational Database Dictionary

Introduction

This dictionary contains more than 600 entries dealing with issues, terms, and concepts involved in, or arising from use of, the relational model of data. Many of the entries include not only definitions but also one or more illustrative examples. I've done my best to make the definitions as clear, precise, and accurate as possible; they're based on my own best understanding of the material, an understanding I've been honing gradually over some 35 years of involvement in this field.

I'd like to stress the point that the dictionary is, as advertised, relational. To that end, I've deliberately omitted terms and concepts that are only tangentially connected to relational matters (e.g., almost all details of the supporting type theory, including type inheritance details in particular). I've also omitted various topics that are part of database technology in general and aren't particular to relational databases (e.g., security issues, the log, recovery and concurrency control, and so forth). What's more, I've also omitted certain SQL terms and concepts that—the fact that SQL is supposed to be a relational language notwithstanding—aren't really relational at all (outer join, UNION ALL, and updating through a cursor are examples). That said, I should add that I have deliberately included a few nonrelational terms in order to make it clear that, contrary to popular opinion, the concepts in question are indeed not relational (*index* is a case in point here).

I must explain too that this is a dictionary with an attitude. It's my very firm belief that the relational model is the right and proper foundation for database technology and will remain so for as far out as anyone can see, and many of the definitions in what follows reflect this belief. As I said in my book *Database in Depth: Relational Theory for Practitioners* (O'Reilly):

> [It's] my opinion that the relational model is rock solid, and "right," and will endure. A hundred years from now, I fully expect database systems still to be based on Codd's relational model. Why? Because the foundations of that model—namely, set theory and predicate logic—are themselves rock solid in turn. Elements of predicate logic in particular go back well over 2000 years, at least as far as Aristotle (384-322 BCE).

In addition, I haven't hesitated to mark some term or concept as deprecated if I believe there are good reasons to avoid it, even if the term or concept in question is in widespread use at the time of writing. *Materialized view* is a case in point here.

The Running Example

The examples that illustrate the definitions are based for the most part on the familiar—not to say hackneyed—suppliers-and-parts database. I apologize for dragging out this old war-horse yet one more time, but I believe that using the same example in a variety of different publications can be a help, not a hindrance, to learning. Here are the relvar definitions (and if you aren't familiar with the term *relvar*, then please check the corresponding dictionary entry!):

```
VAR S BASE RELATION
  { S# S#, SNAME NAME, STATUS INTEGER, CITY CHAR }
    KEY { S# } ;

VAR P BASE RELATION
  { P# P#, PNAME NAME, COLOR COLOR,
                    WEIGHT WEIGHT, CITY CHAR }
    KEY { P# } ;
```

```
VAR SP BASE RELATION
  { S# S#, P# P#, QTY QTY }
    KEY { S#, P# } ;
```

The semantics are as follows:

Relvar S
>Represents suppliers under contract. Each supplier has one supplier number (S#), unique to that supplier; one name (SNAME), not necessarily unique; one status value (STATUS); and one location (CITY). Attributes S#, SNAME, STATUS, and CITY are of types S#, NAME, INTEGER, and CHAR, respectively.

Relvar P
>Represents kinds of parts. Each kind of part has one part number (P#), which is unique; one name (PNAME); one color (COLOR); one weight (WEIGHT); and one location where parts of that kind are stored (CITY). Attributes P#, PNAME, COLOR, WEIGHT, and CITY are of types P#, NAME, COLOR, WEIGHT, and CHAR, respectively.

Relvar SP
>Represents shipments (it shows which parts are shipped, or supplied, by which suppliers). Each shipment has one supplier number (S#), one part number (P#), and one quantity (QTY); there is at most one shipment at any given time for a given supplier and given part. Attributes S#, P#, and QTY are of types S#, P#, and QTY, respectively.

Figure 1 shows a set of sample values. Examples in the body of the dictionary assume these specific values, where it makes any difference.

Alphabetization

For alphabetization purposes, I've followed these rules:

- Punctuation symbols (hyphens, underscores, etc.) are treated as blanks.
- Uppercase precedes lowercase.

S

S#	SNAME	STATUS	CITY
S1	Smith	20	London
S2	Jones	10	Paris
S3	Blake	30	Paris
S4	Clark	20	London
S5	Adams	30	Athens

P

P#	PNAME	COLOR	WEIGHT	CITY
P1	Nut	Red	12.0	London
P2	Bolt	Green	17.0	Paris
P3	Screw	Blue	17.0	Oslo
P4	Screw	Red	14.0	London
P5	Cam	Blue	12.0	Paris
P6	Cog	Red	19.0	London

SP

S#	P#	QTY
S1	P1	300
S1	P2	200
S1	P3	400
S1	P4	200
S1	P5	100
S1	P6	100
S2	P1	300
S2	P2	400
S3	P2	200
S4	P2	200
S4	P4	300
S4	P5	400

Figure 1. The supplier-and-parts database—sample values

- Numerals precede letters.
- Blanks precede everything else.

Technical Issues

The following list summarizes key technical issues underlying the presentation of terms, concepts, and examples in the dictionary:

1. Keywords, variable names, and the like are set in all uppercase throughout.

2. Coding examples are expressed (mostly) in a language called **Tutorial D**. I believe those examples are reasonably self-explanatory, but in any case the **Tutorial D** language is largely defined in the dictionary itself, in the entries for the various relational operators (union, join, restriction, etc.). If needed, a comprehensive description of the language can be found in the book *Databases, Types, and the Relational Model: The Third Manifesto*, Third Edition, by C. J. Date and Hugh Darwen (Addison-Wesley). *Note*: As the subtitle indicates, that book also introduces and explains *The Third Manifesto*, a precise

though somewhat formal definition of the relational model and a supporting type theory (including a comprehensive model of type inheritance). In particular, it uses the name **D** as a generic name for any language that conforms to the principles laid down by *The Third Manifesto*. Any number of distinct languages could qualify as a valid **D**; sadly, however, SQL isn't one of them, which is why examples in this dictionary are expressed in **Tutorial D** and not SQL. (**Tutorial D** is, of course, a valid **D**.)

3. Following on from the previous point, I should make it clear that all relational definitions in this dictionary are intended to conform fully to the relational model as defined by *The Third Manifesto*. Consequently, you might find certain aspects of those definitions a trifle surprising—for example, the assertion in the entry for *deferred checking* that such checking is logically flawed. As I've already said, this is a dictionary with an attitude.

4. It has become standard practice in the industry to use terms such as *projection* and *join* (and so on) in two somewhat different senses: they're used to refer both to the operators identified by those names and also to the results obtained when those operators are invoked. I've followed this practice myself in this dictionary on occasion, and hope it won't lead to confusion.

5. It has become standard practice to interpret the terms *projection* and *join* (and so on) in another sense as well. By definition, these operators apply to relation values specifically. In particular, of course, they apply to the values that happen to be the current values of relvars. It thus clearly makes sense to talk about, for example, the projection on attribute A of relvar R, meaning the relation that results from taking the projection on that attribute A of the current value r of that relvar R. In some contexts, however (normalization, for example), it is convenient to use expressions such as "the projection on attribute A of relvar R" in a slightly different sense. To be specific, we might say, loosely but very conveniently, that

some *relvar* (*RA*, say) is the projection on attribute *A* of relvar *R*—meaning, more precisely, that the value of *RA* at all times is the projection on *A* of the value of *R* at the time in question. In a sense, therefore, we can talk in terms of projections of relvars per se, rather than just in terms of projections of current values of relvars. Analogous remarks apply to all of the relational operations.

6. Certain definitions (of certain operators, for example) require certain values to be of certain specific types. For simplicity, I haven't bothered to spell out this fact in detail in every case but have simply assumed the requirement is satisfied wherever necessary.

7. Several definitions and examples make use of a simplified notation for tuples. For example, consider the SP tuple shown in Figure 1 for supplier S1 and part P1. A formal **Tutorial D** representation of that tuple might look like this:

```
TUPLE { S# S#('S1'), P# P#('P1'), QTY QTY(300) }
```

In the simplified notation under discussion, however, the same tuple would be represented as:

```
<S1,P1,300>
```

8. The notion of *set* is ubiquitous in the database world. On paper, a set is usually represented by a comma-separated list (or *commalist*) of symbols denoting the elements, enclosed in braces as here: {*a,b,c*}. In what follows, therefore, I use braces to enclose commalists of items when the items in question are meant to denote the elements of some set, implying among other things that (a) the order in which the items appear within that commalist is immaterial, and (b) if an item appears more than once, it's treated as if it appeared only once.

9. The notion of *logic* is also ubiquitous in the database world. The relational model in particular is firmly based on logic. More precisely, it's based on conventional two-valued predicate logic, 2VL (q.v.), and all references to

logic in this dictionary should be taken as referring to that logic specifically, except where the context demands otherwise.

10. Continuing from the previous point, many of the entries in this dictionary have to do with concepts from logic. Unfortunately, logic texts (and logicians) vary widely not only in the terminology they use but also, in some cases, in the substance of their definitions. The definitions I give are the ones I find most appropriate myself, but be warned that they're sometimes at odds with others you can find in the literature.

Acknowledgments

This dictionary was Jonathan Gennick's brainchild. Indeed, Jonathan originally intended to write it himself, and I'm very grateful to him for stepping out of the limelight, as it were, and letting me steal his idea and run with it as I've done. Jonathan and I have very different writing styles, and what follows is no doubt a long way from what he originally had in mind, but I hope it at least does justice to his overall idea. I'd also like to thank Jonathan and my other technical reviewers, Hugh Darwen and Nick Tindall, for their many helpful comments on earlier drafts; Hugh in particular had something useful to say on nearly every entry. Needless to say, however, any remaining errors or infelicities are my own responsibility. Finally, I'd like to thank the team at O'Reilly, especially Debby Russell (acquisitions editor), Rachel Monaghan (production editor), and Marlowe Shaeffer (production manager) for their professionalism and their efforts in getting this book out so expeditiously. It has been a pleasure to work with them.

—C. J. Date
Healdsburg, California
August 2006

The Dictionary

0-adic Niladic.

0-tuple The empty tuple.

1NF First normal form.

2NF Second normal form.

2VL Two-valued logic.

3NF Third normal form.

3VL Three-valued logic.

4NF Fourth normal form.

5NF Fifth normal form.

6NF Sixth normal form.

A A relationally complete, "reduced instruction set" version of relational algebra with only two operators—REMOVE (essentially projection over all attributes but one) and an algebraic analog of either NAND or NOR, q.v. The name is a doubly recursive acronym: it stands for *ALGEBRA*, which in turn stands for *A Logical Genesis Explains Basic Relational Algebra*. As this expanded name suggests, it is designed in such a way as to emphasize its close relationship to, and solid foundation in, the discipline of predicate logic, q.v.

ad hoc polymorphism Overloading.

aggregate operator A read-only operator that derives a single value (typically but not necessarily scalar) from the set or bag of values appearing as values of some attribute of some relation. *Contrast* **summary**. *Note*: If (a) the argument to some aggregate operator invocation is empty, and (b) that aggregate operator is essentially just shorthand for repeated invocation of some scalar operator (e.g., the scalar operator is "+" in the case of the aggregate operator SUM), and (c) an identity value exists for that scalar operator (the identity value is 0 in the case of "+"), then the result of that invocation is that identity value.

Example: Let ST be a variable of type INTEGER. Then the following statement assigns to ST the sum of the status values for suppliers in London:

```
ST := SUM ( S WHERE CITY = 'London', STATUS ) ;
```

ALGEBRA *See* A.

algebra 1. Generically, a formal system consisting of a set of objects and a set of operators that together satisfy certain laws and properties (certainly closure, probably commutativity and associativity, and so on). The word algebra itself derives from Arabic *al-jebr*, meaning a resetting (of something broken) or a combination. 2. Relational algebra specifically (if the context demands).

alias Deprecated term used in some SQL products to mean either a tuple calculus range variable or the name of such a variable. The term *table alias* (also deprecated) is also sometimes used with the same meaning.

ALL BUT *See* projection.

ALPHA A proposal, due to Codd, for a concrete relational language based on tuple calculus; also known as Data Sublanguage ALPHA. ALPHA was never implemented, but its ideas were influential on the design of QUEL and (to a much lesser extent) SQL.

alternate key Loosely, a candidate key that isn't the primary key. More precisely, let relvar *R* have primary key *PK*; then *AK* is an alternate key for *R* if and only if *AK* is a candidate key for *R* that isn't *PK*. The term isn't much used.

AND *See* conjunction.

appearance *(Of a value)* An occurrence of a value (in some context). Observe that there's a logical difference between a value as such and an appearance of that value—for example, an appearance as the current value of some variable or as some attribute value within the current value of some tuplevar or relvar. Each such appearance consists internally of some physical representation of the value in question (and distinct appearances of the same value might have distinct physical representations). Thus, there's also a logical difference between an appearance of a value, on the one hand, and the physical representation of that appearance, on the other; there might even be a logical difference between the physical representations used for distinct appearances of the same value. All of that said, however, it's common to abbreviate *physical representation of an appearance of a value* to just *appearance of a value*, or (more often) simply *value*, as long as there's no risk of ambiguity in doing so. Note that *appearance of a value* is a model concept, whereas *physical representation of an appearance* is an implementation concept—users certainly might need to know whether two variables contain appearances of the same value, but they don't need to know whether those appearances use the same physical representation.

Example: Let N1 and N2 be variables of type INTEGER. After the following assignments, then, N1 and N2 both contain an appearance of the integer value 3. The corresponding physical representations might or might not be the same (for example, N1 might use a binary representation and N2 a packed decimal representation), but it's of no concern to the user either way.

```
N1 := 3 ;
N2 := 3 ;
```

argument An actual operand that replaces some parameter of some operator when that operator is invoked. The operand is either a value (denoted by some expression—possibly just a variable reference) or, if and only if the parameter in question is subject to update, a variable (denoted by some variable reference). *Contrast* **parameter**.

Examples: Let operator DOUBLE be defined as follows:

```
OPERATOR DOUBLE ( X INTEGER ) RETURNS INTEGER ;
   RETURN ( 2 * X ) ;
END OPERATOR ;
```

Here, X is a parameter of declared type INTEGER. Let N be a variable of type INTEGER. Then, for example, DOUBLE(N+1) is an invocation of DOUBLE, and the value of the expression N+1 at the time of that invocation is an argument to that invocation. That invocation is itself an expression in turn, and it can appear wherever an integer literal can appear (because operator DOUBLE is defined to return a value of type INTEGER).

Now suppose DOUBLE is defined as an update operator instead of a read-only one:

```
OPERATOR DOUBLE ( X INTEGER ) UPDATES { X } ;
    X := 2 * X ;
END OPERATOR ;
```

Now the parameter X is subject to update, and any argument corresponding to X must be a variable. Thus, e.g., DOUBLE(N) is a valid invocation of DOUBLE, and the variable N—not the value of that variable—is the argument to that invocation. (Note that, for example, DOUBLE(N+1) would be a syntax error, because N+1 isn't a variable reference.) However, that invocation DOUBLE(N) isn't an expression, and it can't appear "wherever an integer literal can appear"; instead, it can appear only in an explicit CALL statement (or equivalent), as here:

```
CALL DOUBLE ( N ) ;
```

arity   Degree. The term isn't used much.

Armstrong's inference rules   *(For FDs)* Let *A, B,* and *C* be arbitrary subsets of the heading of some given relvar. Let *AC* denote the set theory union of *A* and *B*, and likewise for *BC*. Then Armstrong's rules (also known as Armstrong's axioms) state that (a) if *A* is a superset of *B*, then $A \to B$ (the reflexivity rule); (b) if $A \to B$, then $AC \to BC$ (the augmentation rule); and (c) if $A \to B$ and $B \to C$, then $A \to C$ (the transitivity rule). These rules are both sound and complete (*see* **completeness**; **soundness**).

Examples: Let *s* be a set of FDs and let *s* include the FD $A \to BC$. Then the FD $A \to B$ is implied by *s* and can easily be derived using Armstrong's rules as follows: (a) $A \to BC$ (given); (b) $BC \to B$ (reflexivity); hence (c) $A \to B$ (transitivity).

By way of a second example, if the set *s* includes the FDs $A \to B$ and $C \to D$, then the FD $AX \to BD$ (where *X* is the set theory difference between *C* and *B*, in that order) is implied by *s*. *Note*: This example, which is due to Darwen, can be regarded as another inference rule. It has the interesting property that the augmentation and transitivity rules, as well as several other rules that are not discussed in detail here, are all special cases.

arrow   *See* functional dependency.

assignment   An operator that assigns a value (denoted by an expression) to a variable (denoted by a variable reference). The value and the variable must be of the same type. *Note*: Every update operator invocation is semantically equivalent to some assignment (possibly a multiple assignment, q.v.).

Assignment Principle, The   After assignment of value v to variable V, the comparison $v = V$ is required to evaluate to TRUE.

associative   Let Op be a dyadic operator, and assume for definiteness that Op is expressed in infix style. Then Op is associative if and only if, for all x, y, and z, $x\ Op\ (y\ Op\ z) = (x\ Op\ y)\ Op\ z$.

Examples: In ordinary arithmetic, addition ("+") is associative, because

$$x + (y + z) = (x + y) + z$$

for all numbers x, y, and z. Likewise, "||" (string concatenation) is associative, because

$$x\ ||\ (y\ ||\ z) = (x\ ||\ y)\ ||\ z$$

for all strings x, y, and z. (We remark in passing that "+" is also commutative, q.v., but "||" is not.) In the same kind of way, UNION and JOIN are associative in relational algebra (by contrast, MINUS is not). Likewise, AND, OR, and EQUIV are associative in logic (by contrast, IMPLIES is not).

associative addressing   Addressing by value instead of position. All addressing is associative in the relational model, implying among other things that pointers (as that term is usually understood) are explicitly rejected.

atomic predicate   A simple predicate.

atomic proposition   A simple proposition.

atomic statement   *(Programming languages)* Syntactically, a statement that contains no other statements nested inside itself (*contrast* **compound statement**); semantically, a statement that is guaranteed either to execute in its entirety or to have no effect, except possibly for returning a status code. All syntactically atomic statements are semantically atomic in the relational model. (The converse isn't true, incidentally; to be specific, multiple assignment, q.v., is semantically but not syntactically atomic.)

atomic value   Old-fashioned and somewhat deprecated term for a scalar value.

attribute   Loosely, a column; more precisely, an <attribute name, type name> pair, though it's common to refer informally to a given attribute by its attribute name alone. (This simplified form is acceptable because the relational model requires attribute names to be unique within the pertinent heading, and those names thus effectively imply the corresponding type names.)

Examples: In the suppliers-and-parts database, (a) the pair <SNAME,NAME> is an attribute of relvar S; (b) the pair <S#,S#> is an attribute of both relvar S and relvar SP. We might also say, more simply but less formally, that (a) SNAME is an attribute of relvar S, and (b) S# is an attribute of both relvar S and relvar SP. These two attributes are of types NAME and S#, respectively.

attribute constraint   An integrity constraint to the effect that a given attribute of a given relvar is declared to be of a given type.

Example: Attribute SNAME of relvar S is declared to be of type NAME—i.e., it's constrained to contain values of type NAME.

attribute extractor   An operator for extracting the value of a specified attribute from a specified tuple.

Example: Let *t* denote the supplier tuple from Figure 1 for supplier S1. Then the following expression extracts the status value from that tuple:

    STATUS FROM t

attribute FROM   *Tutorial D* syntax for an attribute extractor (q.v.).

attribute renaming   *See* renaming.

attribute type   *See* attribute.

attribute value   *See* tuple value.

augmentation   *See* Armstrong's inference rules.

axiom Something assumed to be true, available for use in the derivation of further truths (i.e., theorems, q.v.). In a database, the tuples in the base relations can be regarded as axioms, because they represent propositions that are assumed to be true. An axiom is a special case of a theorem.

Example: The tuple <S1,Smith,20,London> in the relation that's the current value of base relvar S represents the (presumably true) proposition "Supplier S1 is under contract, is named Smith, has status 20, and is located in London."

bag Very loosely, a "set" that permits duplicates; more precisely, a collection of objects, called elements, in which the same element can appear any number of times.

Example: The collection (b,b,a,c,b,c); equivalently, the collection (a,b,b,b,c,c).

base relation The value of a given base relvar at a given time. *Contrast* **derived relation**.

Examples: The relations that are the values of relvars S, P, and SP at any given time.

base relvar A relvar that is not defined in terms of others; i.e., an independent relvar. *Contrast* **derived relvar**. *Note*: It's a popular misconception that base relvars are physically stored, in the sense that they're represented in storage by physical files, and their tuples and attributes are represented in storage by records and fields within those files (*see* **direct image**). But the relational model deliberately has nothing to say about physical storage; in particular, it categorically doesn't say that base relvars, as such, are physically stored (neither in the foregoing sense, nor in any other). The only requirement is that there must be some defined correspondence between what's physically stored and what's perceived by the user (i.e., base relvars or derived relvars or a mixture of both).

Examples: Relvars S, P, and SP.

base table SQL analog of either a base relation or a base relvar, as the context demands. *See also* **table**.

BCNF Boyce/Codd normal form.

BI-IMPLIES Same as EQUIV.

---

bijection A mapping, or function, from set *s1* to set *s2* such that each element of *s2* is the image of exactly one element of *s1*; equivalently, a mapping that is both an injection and a surjection (in other words, a one-to-one correspondence, in the strict sense of that term, from *s1* to *s2*). Also known as a bijective or "one-to-one onto" mapping. Note that if a given mapping is bijective, then it has an inverse mapping that's bijective as well.

Example: The mapping from integers *x* to their successors *x*+1 is a bijection from the set of all integers to itself, and so is the inverse mapping from integers *x* to their predecessors *x*-1.

binary Of degree two.

body A set of tuples that are all of the same type; more specifically, the set of tuples appearing in a given relation, or in a given relvar at a given time. Every subset of a body is itself a body.

Examples: The set of tuples appearing in relvar S at any given time; any subset of that set.

BOOLEAN A scalar data type (the only one required by the relational model) that contains just the two truth values TRUE and FALSE.

boolean expression An expression denoting a truth value.

boolean value TRUE or FALSE.

bound variable In logic, a variable—more precisely, an occurrence within a predicate of a variable reference—that either (a) appears within the scope of a quantifier that explicitly specifies that variable, or (b) is that explicit specification itself. (The term *variable* is used here in the sense of logic, not in the programming language sense.) *Contrast* **free variable**.

Examples: Let the symbols *x* and *y* denote integers. Then the following expressions are both predicates, and *x* appears as a bound variable, twice, in each of them:

```
EXISTS x ( x > 3 )
EXISTS x ( x > 3 ) AND y < 7
```

The first of these predicates is in fact a proposition, and its meaning is: "There exists an integer *x* such that *x* is greater than three" (a proposition that evaluates to TRUE, of course).

By contrast, the second predicate is not a proposition, because it involves a free variable (namely, y) as well as the two bound ones; thus, it has no truth value.

Turning to a database example, the following is a query ("Get suppliers who supply at least one part") on the suppliers-and-parts database, expressed in tuple calculus, q.v.:

```
S WHERE EXISTS SP ( SP.S# = S.S# )
```

The expression following the keyword WHERE here is a predicate, and the references to SP in that predicate are bound (by contrast, the reference to S is free). Note, however, that in this particular example, the symbols S and SP denote not only variables in the sense of logic but also variables in the conventional programming language sense—but that's because we've indulged in a certain sleight of hand, as it were. Here's an extended version of the same example that should help to clarify matters:

```
SX  RANGES OVER { S }  ;
SPX RANGES OVER { SP } ;

SX WHERE EXISTS SPX ( SPX.S# = SX.S# )
```

Here SX and SPX have been explicitly declared as variables in the sense of logic, ranging over (the current values of) relvars S and SP, respectively. Now it's the references to SPX that are bound and the reference to SX that's free. In effect, what happened in the first version of the example was that we were appealing to a syntax rule that allowed a relvar name to be used to denote an implicitly defined range variable that ranges over (the current value of) the relvar with the same name. We remark that SQL includes a rule of exactly this kind.

Boyce/Codd normal form Relvar R is in Boyce/Codd normal form (BCNF) if and only if for every nontrivial FD $A \rightarrow B$ satisfied by R, A is a superkey for R; equivalently, if and only if every nontrivial FD satisfied by R is implied by some superkey of R. Every BCNF relvar is in 3NF. *Note*: BCNF is "the" normal form with respect to FDs. Also, although being in BCNF clearly doesn't preclude being in the next higher normal form (4NF) as well, the term *BCNF* is often used loosely to refer to a relvar that's in BCNF and not in 4NF.

Example: With the normal forms, it's often more instructive to show a counterexample rather than an example per se. Suppose, therefore, that relvar SP has an additional attribute SNAME, representing the name of the applicable supplier; suppose also that supplier names are necessarily unique (i.e., no two suppliers ever have the same name at the same time). This revised version of SP has two keys, {S#,P#} and {SNAME,P#}, and every subset of the heading—{QTY} in particular—is, of course, functionally dependent on both of them. However, the relvar also satisfies the FDs {S#} → {SNAME} and {SNAME} → {S#}; these FDs are certainly not trivial, nor are they "arrows out of superkeys," so the relvar isn't in BCNF (though it is in 3NF).

business rule *See* relvar predicate.

calculus 1. Generically, a system of formal computation. (The Latin word *calculus* means a pebble, perhaps used in counting or some other form of reckoning.) 2. Relational calculus specifically (if the context demands).

candidate key Loosely, a unique identifier. More precisely, let K be a subset of the heading of relvar R; then K is a candidate key (key for short) for R if and only if (a) no possible value for R contains two distinct tuples with the same value for K (the uniqueness property), while (b) the same can't be said for any proper subset of K (the irreducibility property). Note that every relvar, base or derived, has at least one key. Note too that, by definition, keys are *sets* of attributes; however, if the set of attributes constituting some key K contains just one attribute A, then it's common (though strictly incorrect) to speak informally of that attribute A per se as being that key.

Examples: In the suppliers-and-parts database, {S#}, {P#}, and {S#,P#} are the sole keys for relvars S, P, and SP, respectively. Note that {SNAME} isn't a key for S, because values of {SNAME} aren't necessarily unique (though the values shown in Figure 1 do happen to be unique). Note too that, for example, {S#,CITY} isn't a key for S either, because although its values are necessarily unique, it isn't irreducible (we could discard the CITY attribute, and what remained would still satisfy the uniqueness property).

canonical form Given a set *s1*, together with a notion of equivalence among the elements of that set, subset *s2* of *s1* is a set of canonical forms for *s1* if and only if every element *x1* in *s1* is equivalent to just one element *x2* in *s2* (and that element *x2* is the canonical form for the element *x1*). Various "interesting" properties that apply to *x1* also apply to *x2*; thus, we can study just the small set *s2*, not the large set *s1*, in order to prove a variety of "interesting" theorems or results.

Example: Let *s1* be the set of nonnegative integers and let any two such integers be equivalent if and only if they leave the same remainder on division by five. Then we can define *s2* to be the set {0,1,2,3,4}. As an example of an "interesting" theorem that applies here, let *x1*, *y1*, and *z1* be any three elements of *s1*, and let their canonical forms in *s2* be *x2*, *y2*, and *z2*, respectively; then the product *y1* ∗ *z1* is equivalent to *x1* if and only if the product *y2* ∗ *z2* is equivalent to *x2*.

cardinality The number of elements in a bag or (especially) set; hence, of a relation, the number of tuples in that relation. Also used (a) of a relvar, to mean the number of tuples in the relation that's the value of that relvar at a given time; (b) of an attribute of a relation or relvar, to mean the cardinality of the set of distinct values of that attribute appearing in that relation or relvar—at a given time, in the case of a relvar. (Of course, the cardinality of attribute *A* of relation *r* is the same as the cardinality of the projection *r*{*A*} of that relation over that attribute; definition (b) here is thus strictly redundant.)

Examples: In Figure 1, (a) the cardinality of the relation that's the current value of relvar SP is 12 (and the cardinality of relvar SP is thus currently 12 also); (b) the cardinality of attribute S# in that relation is 4 (and the cardinality of that attribute in relvar SP is thus currently 4 also).

cartesian product 1. *(Dyadic case)* The cartesian product of two relations *r1* and *r2, r1* TIMES *r2*, where *r1* and *r2* have no attribute names in common, is a relation with heading the set theory union of the headings of *r1* and *r2* and with body the set of all tuples *t* such that *t* is the set theory union of a tuple from *r1* and a tuple from *r2*. 2. *(N-adic case)* The cartesian product of *n* relations *r1*, *r2*, ..., *rn* (*n*≥0), TIMES {*r1,r2,...,rn*}, where no two of *r1*, *r2*, ..., *rn* have any attribute names in common, is a relation with heading the set theory union of the headings of *r1, r2, ..., rn* and with body the set of all tuples *t* such that *t* is the set theory union of a tuple from *r1*, a tuple from *r2*, ..., and a tuple from *rn*. *Note:* The relational cartesian product operator differs in several respects from the mathematical operator of the same name (and is sometimes explicitly said to be an expanded, or extended, cartesian product for that reason). In fact, it's a special case of join, q.v.

Example: Let *r1* and *r2* be the projections S{S#} and P{P#}, respectively. Then the cartesian product *r1* TIMES *r2* contains all possible tuples of the form <s#,p#>, where *s#* is an S# value currently appearing in relvar S and *p#* is a P# value currently appearing in relvar P, and no other tuples. (Given the values in Figure 1, the result has cardinality 30.) Note that the expression (S{S#}) TIMES (P{P#}) is semantically equivalent to the expression (S{S#}) JOIN (P{P#}).

catalog Within a given database, a set of relvars that describe that database (including the catalog relvars themselves—i.e., the catalog is self-describing). Such relvars are sometimes said to contain metadata, q.v. Catalog relvars are usually updated not by explicit assignment operations but rather by more user-friendly data definition operators, q.v. (which are nevertheless essentially just shorthand for certain relational assignments).

closed WFF A WFF that denotes a proposition.

Closed World Assumption, The The assumption that (a) if a given tuple appears in a given relvar at a given time, then the proposition represented by that tuple is true at that time, and (b) if a given tuple could appear in that relvar at that time but doesn't, then the proposition represented by that tuple is false at that time. At any given time, in other words, the relvar contains all and only those tuples that correspond to true propositions—that is, invocations, or instantiations, of the relvar predicate that evaluate to TRUE—at that time. *Note:* The foregoing definition is phrased in terms of a relvar specifically. However, a precisely analogous definition applies to relations also.

Examples: The tuple <S1,P1,300> currently appears in relvar SP; we can therefore assume that it currently is the case that supplier S1 supplies part P1 in quantity 300. By contrast, the tuple <S5,P6,250> doesn't currently appear, though presumably it could; we can therefore assume that it's not currently the case that supplier S5 supplies part P6 in quantity 250.

closure 1. *(Of a set of attributes)* The set of all attributes *A* such that the set {*A*} is functionally dependent on the given set. 2. *(Of a set of FDs)* The set of all FDs implied by the given set. 3. *(Of relational algebra)* The property that the result of every algebraic operation is a relation.

closure, transitive *See* transitive closure.

CNF Conjunctive normal form.

Codd, E. F. The inventor of the relational model. See especially his papers (a) "Derivability, Redundancy, and Consistency of Relations Stored in Large Data Banks," IBM Research Report RJ599, August 19th, 1969 (the very first publication on the relational model); (b) "A Relational Model of Data for Large Shared Data Banks," *CACM 13*, No. 6, June 1970 (a revised and extended version of that first paper); and (c) "Relational Completeness of Data Base Sublanguages," in Randall Rustin (ed.), *Data Base Systems*: Courant Computer Science Symposia 6, Prentice Hall (1972). The last of these papers in particular contains formal definitions of tuple calculus and Codd's original relational algebra, also of Codd's reduction algorithm, q.v.

Codd's reduction algorithm An algorithm for reducing an arbitrary tuple calculus expression to a semantically equivalent relational algebra expression. Among other things, the algorithm relies on the fact that the operators projection and division are algebraic counterparts to the existential quantifier and the universal quantifier, respectively, of tuple calculus.

codomain *See* function.

coercion Implicit type conversion (usually best avoided).

column 1. SQL analog of (a) an attribute of some relvar, or (b) an attribute of some relation, or (c) the bag of values of some attribute of some relation, or sometimes even (d) an attribute of some tuple, or (e) the value of some attribute of some tuple (as the context demands). 2. More generally, a picture of an attribute (on paper, for example). *See also* **table**.

commutative Let *Op* be a dyadic operator, and assume for definiteness that *Op* is expressed in infix style. Then *Op* is commutative if and only if, for all x and y, $x\ Op\ y = y\ Op\ x$.

Examples: In ordinary arithmetic, addition ("+") is commutative, because

```
x + y = y + x
```

for all x and y. In the same kind of way, UNION and JOIN are commutative in relational algebra (by contrast, MINUS is not). Likewise, AND, OR, and EQUIV are commutative in logic (by contrast, IMPLIES is not). *Note*: It so happens that all of the operators just mentioned are not only commutative but associative. An example of an operator that's commutative but not associative is NOR, q.v.

comparison A boolean expression of the form (*exp1*) *theta* (*exp2*), where *exp1* and *exp2* are expressions of the same type *T* and *theta* is any comparison operator that makes sense for values of type *T* (certainly "=" or "≠", perhaps ">" also, and so on). *Note*: The parentheses enclosing *exp1* and *exp2* in the comparison might not be needed in practice.

complement *(Of a relation)* Let *r* be a relation with heading {*H*} and body {*b*}. Then the complement of *r* is the unique relation with heading {*H*} and body consisting of all tuples with heading {*H*} that don't appear in {*b*}.

complement (set theory) The set of all elements not appearing in a given set.

completeness *(Not to be confused with relational completeness, q.v.)* The property of a formal system according to which, given a set *s* of sentences of the system, all sentences implied by those in *s* can be derived using the rules of inference of that system (i.e., all tautologies are theorems). *Contrast* soundness.

component *(Of a tuple)* See tuple component.

composite attribute Deprecated term for a combination of two or more attributes. The term is deprecated because a "composite attribute" isn't actually an attribute at all.

composition The composition of relations *r1* and *r2, r1* COMPOSE *r2*, is the join of *r1* and *r2*, projected over all attributes not common to *r1* and *r2*. *See also* **tuple composition**.

Example: Consider the expression S COMPOSE SP. If the current values of relvars S and SP are *s* and *sp*, respectively, this expression yields a relation of type RELATION {SNAME NAME, STATUS INTEGER, CITY CHAR, P# P#, QTY QTY}, with body consisting of all tuples of the form <*n,st,c,p#,q*> such that there exists some supplier number *s#* such that the tuple <*s#,n,st,c*> appears in *s* and the tuple <*s#,p#,q*> appears in *sp*.

compound predicate A predicate that involves at least one connective.

compound proposition A proposition that involves at least one connective.

compound statement Syntactically, a statement that isn't atomic; i.e., a statement that contains other statements nested inside itself.

Examples: Conventional IF, DO, WHILE, and CASE statements; BEGIN …END … statement blocks; and many others.

conditional expression A boolean expression.

conjunct A predicate that's ANDed with zero or more others.

conjunction If *p* and *q* are predicates, their conjunction (*p*) AND (*q*) is a predicate also. Let (*pi*) AND (*qi*) be an invocation of that predicate (where *pi* and *qi* are invocations of *p* and *q*, respectively). Then that invocation (*pi*) AND (*qi*) evaluates to TRUE if and only if *pi* and *qi* both evaluate to TRUE. *Note*: The parentheses enclosing *p* and *q* in the conjunction might not be needed in practice.

conjunctive normal form A predicate is in conjunctive normal form, CNF, if and only if it's of the form (*p1*) AND (*p2*) AND … AND (*pn*), where none of the conjuncts (*p1*), (*p2*), …, (*pn*) involves any ANDs.

connective A monadic or dyadic logical operator. There are exactly 20 connectives in two-valued logic, 4 monadic and 16 dyadic. The most commonly encountered ones are NOT (negation), AND (conjunction), OR (disjunction), IMPLIES (implication), and EQUIV (equivalence); others include NAND, NOR, and XOR, q.v. *Note*: A variety of other symbols and keywords are also used to denote these connectives.

consistency Integrity. *Contrast* consistency.

consistent *(Of a database)* Satisfying all defined integrity constraints.

constraint An integrity constraint.

contradiction A predicate whose every possible invocation is guaranteed to yield FALSE, regardless of what arguments are substituted for its parameters. *Contrast* tautology.

Examples: Let *p1* be the predicate (actually a proposition) $2+2 = 5$; let *p2* be the predicate $x > x$, where x is an arbitrary integer; and let *p3* be the predicate (p) AND $(NOT(p))$, where p is an arbitrary predicate. Then *p1, p2,* and *p3* are all contradictions.

controlled redundancy Redundancy (q.v.) is controlled if it does exist (and the user is aware of it), but the task of "propagating updates" to ensure that it never leads to any inconsistencies is managed by the DBMS, not the user. Uncontrolled redundancy can be a problem, but controlled redundancy shouldn't be. As a general rule, databases shouldn't include any uncontrolled redundancy.

correct *See* correctness.

correctness *(Of a database)* The property of truly reflecting the state of affairs that exists in the real world. *Contrast* consistency.

correlation name SQL term for either a tuple calculus range variable or the name of such a variable.

cover *(Of a set of FDs)* If *s1* and *s2* are sets of FDs, then *s2* is a cover for *s1* if and only if every FD implied by *s1* is implied by *s2*. *Note*: Some writers use the term *cover* in a stronger sense, to mean a set of FDs that's equivalent to some given set. *See* equivalence.

cross join / cross product Cartesian product.

CWA The Closed World Assumption.

D_UNION *See* disjoint union.

data definition operator An operator that either (a) defines some database object, such as a base relvar or a view or a snapshot or a constraint, or (b) deletes or updates such a definition; in other words, an operator that updates the catalog.

Examples: See the definitions of relvars S, P, and SP. Other examples could be (a) an operation to add an attribute to one of those relvars, or (b) an operation to define a constraint on those relvars, or (c) an operation to drop one of those relvars or a constraint entirely.

data independence 1. *(Physical)* The ability to change the physical design of a database without having to make corresponding changes in the way the database is perceived by users. 2. *(Logical)* The ability to change the logical design of a database without having to make corresponding changes in the way the database is perceived by users.

data manipulation operator Loosely, an operator that isn't a data definition operator. However, the distinction isn't hard and fast; in fact, it's difficult to find an operator that doesn't, in the final analysis, "manipulate" data of some kind (unless it's a read-only operator, possibly; some authorities might argue that only update operators "manipulate" data). The term is probably best avoided.

data model 1. An abstract, self-contained, logical definition of the data structures, data operators, and so forth, that together make up the abstract machine with which users interact (*contrast* **implementation**). 2. A model of the persistent data of some particular enterprise (i.e., a logical database design).

Examples: The most obvious example of the first definition is the relational model. Note that we can sum up the distinction between a data model in this first sense and an implementation of that model by saying that the model is what the user has to know, while the implementation is what the user doesn't have to know. As for the second definition, any logical database design will suffice as an example.

data sublanguage A language that provides database support for one or more distinct host languages (q.v.) in which it can be embedded or from which it can be invoked.

Data Sublanguage ALPHA *See* ALPHA.

---

data type Type.

database Strictly, a database value, q.v.; more commonly used, in this dictionary in particular, to refer to what would more accurately be called a database variable, q.v. We assume throughout this dictionary that databases are always relational, barring explicit statements to the contrary. *Note*: The term *database* is also used in nonrelational contexts to mean a variety of other things: for example, a collection of physically stored data. It's also used, all too frequently, to mean a DBMS, but this particular usage is strongly deprecated. (If we call the DBMS a database, what do we call the database?)

database constraint 1. *("A" database constraint)* An integrity constraint that isn't a type constraint; informally, an integrity constraint that refers to two or more distinct relvars. 2. *("The" database constraint)* The logical AND of all integrity constraints, apart from type constraints, that apply to a given database (*the* database constraint—sometimes called the *total* database constraint—for the database in question).

Examples: First, the key and foreign key constraints specified in the definition of the suppliers-and-parts database are all database constraints. Second, here are some more database constraints that might apply to that database:

```
CONSTRAINT C1 IS_EMPTY
   ( S WHERE STATUS < 1 OR STATUS > 100 ) ;
/* status values must be in the */
/* range 1 to 100 inclusive     */

CONSTRAINT C2 IS_EMPTY
   ( P WHERE CITY = 'London' AND COLOR ≠ 'Red' ) ;
/* parts in London must be red */

CONSTRAINT C3 IS_EMPTY
   ( ( S JOIN SP )
     WHERE STATUS < 20 AND P# = P#('P6') ) ;
/* no supplier with status less */
/* than 20 can supply part P6    */
```

Finally, suppose for the sake of the example that the specified key and foreign key constraints, together with constraints C1-C3, are the only database constraints that apply to the suppliers-and-parts database. Then the logical AND of all of them is "the" (total) database constraint for that database.

database design   *See* logical database design; physical database design.

database management system   The software system (the DBMS) that controls all access to some database or collection of databases. *Contrast* database.

database programming language   A programming language that includes fully integrated ("native") database support. *Contrast* data sublanguage; host language.

database value   A possible "state" for some database; i.e., a collection of relations, those relations being possible values for the applicable relvars. Conceptually, therefore, a database value can be thought of as a set of propositions, those propositions corresponding to the tuples in the applicable relations. *Contrast* database variable.

Example: The relations (i.e., relation values) shown in Figure 1 constitute the "state" of the suppliers-and-parts database that happens to be current at some particular time. But if we were to look at that database at some different time, we would probably see a different state. In other words, the database is really a variable—a database variable, to be precise, meaning a variable whose values are database values. Moreover, the tuples in the relations that are the values of relvars S, P, and SP at any given time represent propositions—propositions that are assumed by convention to be true at that time, so the database at the time in question can be thought of as a set of true propositions.

database variable   Loosely, a container for relvars; more accurately, a variable whose value at any given time is a database value. Strictly speaking, there's a logical difference, precisely analogous to that between relation values and relation variables, between database values and database variables. To be specific, what we usually call a database is really a variable (typically a rather large one), and updating that database has the effect of replacing one value of that variable by another—where the values in question are database values and the variable is a database variable. More precisely still, a database is a tuple variable, with one attribute (relation-valued) for each relvar in the database in question. Note, therefore, that a database variable isn't really a set of relation variables, even though we often think of it that way informally. All of that said, however, we bow to traditional usage elsewhere in this dictionary and use the term *database* to refer to both database values and database variables, relying on context to make it clear which is intended.

Example: *See* **database value**. As for the matter of a database really being a tuple variable, the suppliers-and-parts database in particular can be thought of as a tuple variable of the following tuple type:

```
TUPLE { S  RELATION { S# S#, SNAME NAME,
                      STATUS INTEGER, CITY CHAR },
        P  RELATION { P# P#, PNAME NAME, COLOR COLOR,
                      WEIGHT WEIGHT, CITY CHAR },
        SP RELATION { S# S#, P# P#, QTY QTY } }
```

DBMS Database Management System; plural DBMSs.

dbvar A database variable.

DCO Domain check override.

De Morgan's Laws 1. *(Logic)* The negation of the disjunction of predicates *p* and *q* is equivalent to the conjunction of the negations of *p* and *q*; the negation of the conjunction of predicates *p* and *q* is equivalent to the disjunction of the negations of *p* and *q*. 2. *(Set theory)* The complement of the union of sets *s1* and *s2* is equal to the intersection of the complements of *s1* and *s2*; the complement of the intersection of sets *s1* and *s2* is equal to the union of the complements of *s1* and *s2*.

decidability The property of a formal system according to which, given an arbitrary sentence *s*, it can be determined whether or not *s* is a sentence of the system. *Note*: Propositional calculus is decidable; predicate calculus is not.

declared type 1. *(Of a value)* The type of the value in question. 2. *(Of a variable or an attribute)* The type specified when the variable or attribute in question is defined. 3. *(Of an expression)* The type of the value denoted by the expression in question. *Note*: The term *declared type* can safely be reduced to *type* if inheritance is not supported.

decomposition Nonloss decomposition (unless the context demands otherwise).

DEE TABLE_DEE.

deferred checking Checking an integrity constraint at some time (typically commit time) later than the time at which an update is performed that might cause it to be violated. The relational model rejects deferred checking as logically flawed. *Contrast* immediate checking.

deferred constraint A constraint for which the checking is deferred (*see* deferred checking). The relational model rejects deferred constraints as logically flawed. *Contrast* immediate constraint.

degree The number n of attributes in a given heading, key, tuple, tuplevar, relation, or relvar ($n \geq 0$).

Examples: The degrees of relvars S, P, and SP are four, five, and three, respectively; the degrees of the corresponding keys are one, one, and two, respectively.

DELETE Loosely, an operator that removes a given set of tuples from a given relvar. It's shorthand for a certain relational assignment.

Example: The DELETE statement

```
DELETE S WHERE CITY = 'Athens' ;
```

is shorthand for the following relational assignment:

```
S := S WHERE NOT ( CITY = 'Athens' ) ;
```

DELETE rule A specific kind of foreign key rule, q.v.

denormalization Replacing a set of relvars *R1, R2, ..., Rn* by their join *R*, such that for all *i* the projection of *R* over the attributes of *Ri* is guaranteed to be equal to *Ri* ($i = 1, 2, ..., n$). *Note*: Denormalization (at least to a level below 5NF) is always contraindicated from a logical point of view. Sometimes it can't be avoided, however, given the level of technology found in today's commercial products.

Example: A denormalization that might be applied to the suppliers-and-parts database would be to replace relvars S and SP by their join (SSP, say). Relvars S and SP could then be derived by projecting relvar SSP over the attributes of S and the attributes of SP, respectively.

dependency An IND or JD or MVD or (especially) FD.

dependency theory A body of theory, built on top of the relational model, that can be used to help with logical database design (though it's not limited to that purpose alone).

dependent In an FD, the set of attributes on the right-hand side. *Contrast* determinant.

Example: In the FD {S#,P#} → {QTY}, which is satisfied by relvar SP, {QTY} is the dependent and {S#,P#} is the determinant.

dereferencing *See* referencing.

derived relation Loosely, a relation defined in terms of others. More precisely, let *s* be a set of relations. Then relation *r* is derived from those in *s* if and only if it doesn't itself appear in *s* but can be obtained (by means of some nonempty sequence of relational operations) from those that do. For the purposes of this definition, (a) the only permitted operations are restriction, projection, join, union, and difference; (b) the only permitted operands are relations in *s* or relations derived from those in *s*. *Contrast* base relation.

Example: Consider the expression S JOIN SP. If the current values of relvars S and SP are *s* and *sp*, respectively, this expression defines the derived relation that is the join of *s* and *sp*.

derived relvar A relvar defined in terms of others (in particular, a view or snapshot, q.v.). *Contrast* base relvar.

determinant In an FD, the set of attributes on the left-hand side. *Contrast* dependent.

difference The difference between two relations *r1* and *r2* (in that order), *r1* MINUS *r2*, where *r1* and *r2* are of the same type *T*, is a relation of type *T* with body the set of all tuples *t* such that *t* appears in *r1* and not *r2*. *Note*: The relational difference operator is a special case of semidifference, q.v.

Example: The expression (S{CITY}) MINUS (P{CITY}) denotes the difference between the projections on CITY of the relations that are the current values of relvars S and P (in that order). That difference is a relation of type RELATION {CITY CHAR}. Moreover, if the current values of relvars S and P are *s* and *p*, respectively, the body of that relation consists of all tuples of the form <c> that appear in s{CITY} and not p{CITY}—meaning c is a current supplier city that isn't also a current part city. Note that the expression (S{CITY}) MINUS (P{CITY}) is semantically equivalent to the expression (S{CITY}) NOT MATCHING (P{CITY})—or the simpler expression (S{CITY}) NOT MATCHING P, for that matter.

difference (set theory) The set of all elements appearing in one given set and not in another. *Contrast* symmetric difference.

direct image A somewhat unsophisticated implementation style, found in most if not all of today's mainstream database products, in which what's physically stored is effectively just a direct image of what the user logically sees (i.e., relvars are stored as physical files, and tuples and attributes are stored as records and fields within those files).

directed relationship A (binary) relationship, in the sense of the third definition of that term.

disjoint Sets *s1* and *s2* are disjoint if and only if they have no elements in common.

disjoint union A version of the relational union operator for which the operand relations are required to be disjoint, meaning they have no tuples in common. (This operation could obviously be generalized to apply to sets in general as well as relations in particular.)

Example: Consider the expression (S{CITY}) D_UNION (P{CITY}). If the current values of relvars S and P are as shown in Figure 1, this expression causes a run-time error, because the operands aren't disjoint. If they were, however, the expression would then be semantically equivalent to (S{CITY}) UNION (P{CITY}).

disjunct A predicate that's ORed with zero or more others.

disjunction If *p* and *q* are predicates, their disjunction (*p*) OR (*q*) is a predicate also. Let (*pi*) OR (*qi*) be an invocation of that predicate (where *pi* and *qi* are invocations of *p* and *q*, respectively). Then that invocation (*pi*) OR (*qi*) evaluates to TRUE if and only if at least one of *pi* and *qi* evaluates to TRUE. *Note*: The parentheses enclosing *p* and *q* in the disjunction might not be needed in practice.

disjunctive normal form   A predicate is in disjunctive normal form, DNF, if and only if it's of the form (*p1*) OR (*p2*) OR ... OR (*pn*), where none of the disjuncts (*p1*), (*p2*), ..., (*pn*) involves any ORs.

distributive   1. Let operators *OpM* and *OpD* be monadic and dyadic, respectively, and assume for definiteness that *OpD* is expressed in infix style. Then *OpM* distributes over *OpD* if and only if, for all *x* and *y*, *OpM*(*x* *OpD* *y*) = (*OpM*(*x*)) *OpD* (*OpM*(*y*)). 2. Let operators *OpC* and *OpD* both be dyadic, and assume for definiteness that they're expressed in infix style. Then *OpC* distributes over *OpD* if and only if, for all *x*, *y*, and *z*, *x* *OpC* (*y* *OpD* *z*) = (*x* *OpC* *y*) *OpD* (*x* *OpC* *z*).

Examples: In ordinary arithmetic, nonnegative square root ("√") distributes over multiplication ("*"), because

$$\surd \; (\; x \; * \; y \;) \; = \; \surd \; (\; x \;) \; * \; \surd \; (\; y \;)$$

for all *x* and *y*; also, multiplication distributes over addition ("+"), because

$$x \; * \; (\; y \; + \; z \;) \; = \; (\; x \; * \; y \;) \; + \; (\; x \; * \; z \;)$$

for all *x*, *y*, and *z*. In the same kind of way, restriction distributes over UNION, INTERSECT, and MINUS, and INTERSECT distributes over UNION, in relational algebra.

DIVIDEBY   *See* division.

division   Let relations *r1, r2,* and *r3* be such that (a) the set {*X*} is the common attributes of *r1* and *r3*; (b) the set {*Y*} is the common attributes of *r2* and *r3*; and (c) the sets {*X*} and {*Y*} are disjoint. Then the division *r1* DIVIDEBY *r2* PER (*r3*)—where *r1* is the dividend, *r2* is the divisor, and *r3* is the "mediator"—is a relation with the same heading as *r1* and with body defined as follows: tuple *t* appears in that body if and only if it appears in *r1*, and a tuple <*x,y*> with *x* equal to the *X* value in *t* appears in *r3*{*X,Y*} for all tuples <*y*> appearing in *r2*{*Y*}. Equivalently, the division *r1* DIVIDEBY *r2* PER (*r3*) is shorthand for the expression *r1* WHERE *r2*{*Y*} ⊆ ((*r3* RENAME (*X* AS *Z*)) WHERE *Z* = *X*){*Y*}. (The expression *Z* = *X* here is a tuple comparison; the expression *r2*{*Y*} ⊆ (...){*Y*} is a relation comparison.) *Note*: The division operator as just defined is sometimes known as the Small Divide. A Great Divide can also be defined, but the details are beyond the scope of this dictionary.

Example: The expression S DIVIDEBY P PER (SP) yields a relation of the same type as relvar S, with body consisting of supplier tuples for suppliers who supply all parts mentioned in relvar P. (Given the sample values of Figure 1, the result contains just the tuple for supplier S1.)

DK/NF Domain-key normal form.

DNF Disjunctive normal form.

domain 1. *(Relational model)* Type. Earlier relational writings favored the term *domain*; more recent ones favor the term *type* instead. 2. *(Mathematics) See* **function**.

domain calculus A version of relational calculus, semantically equivalent to tuple calculus (q.v.), in which the range variables range over domains (types) instead of relations and thus denote values from those domains.

Example: Here's a domain calculus formulation of the query "Get supplier names for suppliers who supply at least one part" (*see* **tuple calculus** for a tuple calculus analog):

```
NX RANGES OVER { NAME } ;
SX RANGES OVER { S# }   ;
PX RANGES OVER { P# }   ;

NX WHERE
   EXISTS SX ( EXISTS PX ( S { S# SX, SNAME NX } AND
                          SP { S# SX, P# PX } ) )
```

In stilted English: "Get names NX where there exists a supplier number SX and there exists a part number PX such that a tuple with supplier number SX and supplier name NX appears in relvar S and a tuple with the same supplier number SX and part number PX appears in relvar SP." As you can see, this particular example is somewhat clumsier than its tuple calculus counterpart (*see* **tuple calculus**), but there are also cases where the reverse is true.

domain check override An ad hoc, flawed, and therefore deprecated mechanism for performing comparisons between values of different types.

domain-key normal form Relvar *R* is in domain-key normal form, DK/NF, if and only if every constraint that applies to *R* is implied by the attribute and key constraints that apply to *R*.

Note: *Attribute-key normal form* would be a better name. In any case, the concept is mainly of academic interest, because relvars can easily fail to be in DK/NF and yet be fully normalized (i.e., in 5NF or even 6NF).

Example: As noted under **Boyce/Codd normal form**, with the normal forms it's often more instructive to show a counterexample rather than an example per se. Suppose, therefore, that shipments satisfy a constraint to the effect that odd-numbered parts can be supplied only by odd-numbered suppliers and even-numbered parts only by even-numbered suppliers (the example is very contrived, of course, but it suffices for the purpose at hand). Then this constraint is clearly not implied by the attribute and key constraints that apply to relvar SP, so SP isn't in DK/NF; yet it's certainly in 6NF.

domain relational calculus Domain calculus.

dot qualification In tuple calculus, a dot-qualified name is an expression of the form *rx.A*, where *rx* is the name of a range variable and *A* is the name of an attribute of the relation *r* over which *rx* ranges. Such an expression serves as an attribute reference; it denotes the value of attribute *A* in the particular tuple of *r* to which *rx* currently refers. Dot qualification is used for disambiguation purposes in tuple calculus—also in SQL—but not in domain calculus or relational algebra (these latter use attribute (re)naming and name scoping to achieve the same purpose).

Example: The following tuple calculus formulation of the query "Get suppliers who supply at least one part" makes use of two dot-qualified names, SPX.S# and SX.S#:

```
SX  RANGES OVER { S } ;
SPX RANGES OVER { SP } ;

SX WHERE EXISTS SPX ( SPX.S# = SX.S# )
```

For comparison, here is a relational algebra formulation of the same query:

```
S MATCHING SP
```

The "matching" here is based on the attribute name "S#", that attribute being the only one common to relvars S and SP.

double arrow *See* multivalued dependency.

double underlining A convention, illustrated in Figure 1, for marking attributes that participate in primary keys.

dual mode principle The principle that any relational operation that can be invoked interactively can also be invoked from an application program.

DRC Domain relational calculus.

DUM TABLE_DUM.

duplicate Let *a1* and *a2* be appearances (q.v.) in some context of values *v1* and *v2*, respectively. Then *a1* and *a2* are duplicates of each other if and only if *v1* and *v2* are equal (in other words, if and only if *v1* and *v2* are the very same value). *Note*: It should be clear from this definition that the well-known dictum to the effect that relations never contain duplicate tuples really means that no relation ever contains duplicate *appearances* of the *same* tuple—though we tend to stay with the less precise formulation in this dictionary for reasons of familiarity. Observe that because (a) relations never contain duplicate tuples and (b) every relational operation yields a relation, it follows that duplicates are eliminated, if necessary, whenever a relational operation is performed (meaning, more precisely, that redundant duplicate tuple appearances are eliminated).

Examples (duplicate elimination): Given the sample values shown in Figure 1, the projection over CITY of the current value of relvar S has cardinality 3, not 5; similarly, the union of the projections over CITY of the current values of relvars S and P has cardinality 4, not 11. (Note that, of the most familiar relational operators, projection and union are the only ones for which duplicate elimination is a concern. For the others—restriction, join, and so on—it's effectively a no op.)

duplicate elimination *See* duplicate.

dyadic *(Of an operator)* Having exactly two operands; i.e., being defined in terms of exactly two parameters.

E/R Entity/relationship.

E/R diagram *See* entity/relationship diagram.

E/R model *See* entity/relationship model.

E/R modeling *See* entity/relationship modeling.

element *See* bag; set.

empty *(Of a bag or set)* Having no elements.

empty foreign key A foreign key of degree zero. *Note*: The matching candidate key in the referenced relvar will necessarily also be of degree zero, and the referential constraint will therefore be satisfied if and only if either (a) the referenced relvar is nonempty, or (b) the referencing relvar is empty (or both).

empty heading The heading of degree zero (note that there's exactly one such).

empty key A key of degree zero. Note that a relvar with an empty key can't have any other keys in addition to the empty one, because of the irreducibility requirement on keys (*see* **candidate key**). Note too that such a relvar can't contain more than one tuple, because otherwise the key constraint would be violated. Declaring relvar *R* to have an empty key is thus a convenient way of imposing the constraint that *R* never has cardinality greater than one.

empty relation A relation of cardinality zero (note that there's exactly one such for each possible relation type).

Example: Suppose relvars S and P are both currently empty; that is, their current values *s* and *p* are both empty relations. Then *s* and *p* aren't equal, even though their bodies are equal, precisely because they're of different types (equivalently, because their headings aren't equal).

empty relvar A relvar whose current value is an empty relation.

empty restriction A restriction of a given relation *r* that contains no tuples (i.e., is equal to *r* WHERE FALSE); in particular, a restriction of the form *r* WHERE *c*, where *c* is a contradiction (q.v.).

Examples: The expressions S WHERE STATUS = 25 and S WHERE STATUS > STATUS are both empty restrictions (the second necessarily so, because STATUS > STATUS is a contradiction).

empty set The set with no elements (note that there's exactly one such). All theorems, properties, definitions, etc., that apply to sets in general apply to the empty set in particular. For example, relation headings and bodies are both defined as sets (of attributes and tuples, respectively), so they are each allowed to be the empty set in particular.

empty tuple   The tuple of degree zero (note that there's exactly one such).

empty type   A type with no values. This concept is of crucial importance if inheritance is supported but is perhaps of little use otherwise.

encapsulated   Scalar. *Note*: The term is also used, especially in OO contexts, to refer to the physical bundling, or packaging, of code and data (or operator definitions and data representation definitions, to be more precise). But to use the term in this way is to mix model and implementation considerations; the user shouldn't care, and shouldn't need to care, whether or not code and data are physically bundled together.

entity   A thing. *Note*: It's frequently suggested that there should be a one-to-one correspondence between "entities of interest" and tuples in base relvars. The suggestion is hard to sustain, however, given that the term *entities of interest* has no precise definition. (Of course, the same is true of the term *entity* itself, for that matter.)

entity integrity   The rule that attributes of primary keys in base relvars don't allow nulls. However, since (a) relvars, base or otherwise, don't necessarily have to have primary keys (*see* **primary key**), and (b) rules that apply to base relvars but not to other kinds are more than a little suspect anyway (because they violate *The Principle of Interchangeability*), the entity integrity rule could be, and in fact has been, dropped without serious loss. We mention it here mainly for historical reasons. In any case, it refers to nulls, which aren't part of the relational model; it would thus require major revision anyway before any suggestion that it be kept could be seriously entertained.

entity/relationship diagram   A picture intended to explicate the logical design of a given database at a level of abstraction in which many details—in particular, details of the underlying types and almost all integrity constraints—are omitted.

entity/relationship model A set of conventions for drawing entity/relationship diagrams, q.v.

entity/relationship modeling The process of using the conventions of the entity/relationship model, q.v., as a tool for assisting in the logical database design process.

equality Two values are equal if and only if they're the very same value. For example, the integer 3 is equal to the integer 3 and not to the integer 4, nor to any other integer (nor to anything else, either). More precisely, let *T* be a type; then the equality operator "=" for values of type *T* is defined as follows. Let *v1* and *v2* be two such values, and let *Op* be an operator with a parameter *x* of type *T*. Then *v1* and *v2* are equal (i.e., *v1* = *v2* evaluates to TRUE) if and only if, for all such operators *Op*, two successful invocations of *Op* that are identical in all respects except that the argument corresponding to *x* is *v1* in one invocation and *v2* in the other are indistinguishable in their effect. *Note*: The equality operator is—in fact, must be—defined for every type. *See* duplicate; overloading; set; set membership; relation equality; tuple equality.

equijoin A theta join in which theta is "=".

EQUIV *See* equivalence.

equivalence 1. *(Of sets of FDs)* Two sets of FDs are equivalent if and only if each is a cover for the other. *Note*: Any given set of FDs always has an equivalent set that's irreducible (*see* irreducible). 2. *(Logic)* If *p* and *q* are predicates, the equivalence (*p*) EQUIV (*q*) is a predicate also. Let (*pi*) EQUIV (*qi*) be an invocation of that predicate (where *pi* and *qi* are invocations of *p* and *q*, respectively). Then that invocation (*pi*) EQUIV (*qi*) evaluates to TRUE if and only if *pi* and *qi* both evaluate to TRUE or both evaluate to FALSE. (In other words, (*p*) EQUIV (*q*) is equivalent to ((*p*) IMPLIES (*q*)) AND ((*q*) IMPLIES (*p*)).) *Note*: The parentheses enclosing *p* and *q* in the expression (*p*) EQUIV (*q*) might not be needed in practice.

essentiality A data structure is essential to a given data model (in the sense of the first definition of that term) if its removal would make some information impossible to represent using that model.

Example: The relational model includes only one data structure, the relation itself; that data structure is clearly essential because if it were removed, the relational model would be incapable of representing anything at all. However, because the relational model is, in fact, capable of representing absolutely any data whatsoever, any data model that supports relations in some shape or form as well as some additional data structure *DS* must be such that either relations are inessential or *DS* is. But if relations are inessential, then *DS* must be logically equivalent to relations!—in which case, it could be argued that it's really *DS* that's inessential anyway, not relations. What's more, a data model that doesn't "support relations in some shape or form" is unlikely in the extreme (even SQL could be said to support relations if various SQL features—nulls, duplicate rows, etc.—are avoided). Thus, for example, pointers (object IDs), bags, lists, and arrays could all be removed from the so-called object model without any loss of representational power. (Indeed, the fact that they're not removed is prima facie evidence that "the object model" fails to distinguish properly between model and implementation issues.)

EXCEPT   Same as MINUS.

exclusive OR   If *p* and *q* are predicates, their exclusive OR (*p*) XOR (*q*) is a predicate also. Let (*pi*) XOR (*qi*) be an invocation of that predicate (where *pi* and *qi* are invocations of *p* and *q*, respectively). Then that invocation (*pi*) XOR (*qi*) evaluates to TRUE if and only if exactly one of *pi* and *qi* evaluates to TRUE. (In other words, (*p*) XOR (*q*) is equivalent to NOT((*p*) EQUIV (*q*)).) *Note*: The parentheses enclosing *p* and *q* in the expression (*p*) XOR (*q*) might not be needed in practice.

existential quantifier   Let *p(x)* be a predicate with a parameter *x*; then EXISTS *x* (*p(x)*) is a predicate, and it means "There exists at least one argument value *v* that can replace the parameter *x* such that *p(v)* is true." In this example, EXISTS *x* is an existential quantifier, and *x* is an existentially quantified bound variable (q.v.). *Note*: Some writers refer to EXISTS by itself as the quantifier; the literature is not consistent on this point. More important, note that if *v1, v2, …, vn* are all of the possible argument values in the foregoing example, then EXISTS *x* (*p(x)*) is equivalent to (*p(v1)*) OR (*p(v2)*) OR … OR (*p(vn)*) OR

FALSE. Observe in particular that this expression evaluates to FALSE if $n = 0$ (i.e., if the bound variable x ranges over an empty set).

Examples: See **bound variable**; **domain calculus**; **free variable**; **tuple calculus**; and elsewhere.

EXISTS *See* **existential quantifier**. In the literature, EXISTS is often represented by a backward E, thus: $\exists$.

expanded cartesian product *See* **cartesian product**.

expressible relation Any relation that, given a particular set of relations, is either included in that set or can be derived from those that are (*see* **derived relation**).

expression In a programming language, a construct that denotes a value; i.e., a rule for computing or determining the value in question. Every expression is of some type: namely, the type of the value it denotes. *Contrast* **statement**.

Example: X+Y is an expression; it denotes the value that's the sum of the current values of the variables X and Y. By contrast,

```
Z := X + Y ;
```

is a statement; it assigns the value denoted by the expression X+Y on the right-hand side to the variable Z referenced on the left-hand side.

expression transformation The process of transforming one expression into another, semantically equivalent expression; applies to relational expressions in particular, where it's sometimes called *query rewrite*. Query rewrite is typically done for performance reasons; it can be done either by the user or, much more importantly, by the system (*see* **optimizer**).

Example: The relational expression (*r* WHERE *br*) JOIN (*s* WHERE *bs*) is semantically equivalent to the relational expression (*r* JOIN *s*) WHERE (*br*) AND (*bs*); therefore, either expression can be transformed into the other. Transforming the second into the first is likely to be advantageous from a performance standpoint, because the first means doing the restrictions before the join; thus, it's likely that the input relations to the join will be smaller and the output will be smaller too. In fact, this transformation could make the difference between keeping the JOIN result in memory and having to spill it out onto the disk.

EXTEND   *See* extension.

extended cartesian product   *See* cartesian product.

Extensible Markup Language   *See* XML.

extension   1. *(Relational algebra)* Let *r* be a relation. Then the extension EXTEND *r* ADD (*exp* AS *X*) is a relation with (a) heading the heading of *r* extended with attribute *X*, and (b) body consisting of all tuples *t* such that *t* is a tuple of *r* extended with a value for attribute *X* that is computed by evaluating the expression *exp* on that tuple of *r*. Relation *r* must not have an attribute called *X*, and *exp* must not refer to *X*. *See also* **tuple extension**. 2. *(Predicate)* Let *p* be a predicate; then the extension of *p* consists of all instantiations of *p* (i.e., all propositions that can be obtained from *p*) that evaluate to TRUE. 3. *(Relation)* Following on from the previous definition, let *r* be a relation. Then the heading of *r* can be regarded as representing a predicate (*see* **relation predicate**), and the body of *r* can be regarded as representing the extension of that predicate. Hence, the term *extension* is also sometimes used to refer to the body of a relation. *Contrast* **intension**.

Example (first definition only): The following expression denotes an extension of the relation that's the current value of relvar P:

```
EXTEND P ADD ( WEIGHT * 454 AS GMWT )
```

That extension is a relation just like the current value of relvar P, except that it has an additional attribute GMWT ("gram weight"), whose value in any given tuple is 454 times the WEIGHT value in that same tuple. Note that relvar P per se remains unaltered in the database—EXTEND isn't like ALTER TABLE in SQL; it's simply a read-only operator that (like restrict, for example) takes a certain relation as input and returns another as output.

external predicate   The relvar predicate for a given relvar. *Contrast* **internal predicate**. *Note*: Since this latter term is deprecated, the term *external predicate* is deprecated (somewhat) as well.

FALSE   *See* boolean value.

FD   Functional dependency.

FD implied by a superkey The FD $A \rightarrow B$ is implied by a superkey if and only if A is a superkey for the pertinent relvar.

FD preservation Decomposing a relvar R into its projections $R1$, $R2$, ..., Rn in such a way that every FD in R is implied by those in $R1$, $R2$, ..., Rn. *Note: R1, R2, ..., Rn* here are said to be *independent projections.*

Example: Suppose relvar S satisfies the additional FD {CITY} $\rightarrow$ {STATUS}; i.e., the status for a given supplier is a function of that supplier's location. Then replacing S by its projections on {S#,SNAME,CITY} and {CITY,STATUS} preserves FDs, because every FD satisfied by S is either satisfied by one of the two projections or is implied by those that are. By contrast, suppose S is replaced by its projections on {S#,SNAME,CITY} and {S#,STATUS} instead. Now the FD {CITY} $\rightarrow$ {STATUS} isn't implied by the FDs satisfied by those projections (even though the decomposition is nonloss). One practical consequence is that updates to either of the two projections must now be monitored (either by the DBMS or, more likely in practice, by some application) to ensure that the FD {CITY} $\rightarrow$ {STATUS} is satisfied; for example, consider what's involved in moving supplier S1 from London to Paris. In other words, the two projections aren't independent in the latter decomposition. Given the level of technology found in today's commercial products, therefore, it's generally preferable to perform decomposition in such a way as to preserve FDs—i.e., to decompose into independent projections—whenever possible.

fifth normal form Relvar R is in fifth normal form, 5NF, if and only if every nontrivial JD satisfied by R is implied by the superkeys of R. Every 5NF relvar is in 4NF. *Note*: 5NF is "the" normal form with respect to JDs. Also, although being in 5NF clearly doesn't preclude being in 6NF as well, the term *5NF* is often used loosely to refer to a relvar that's in 5NF and not in 6NF.

Example: As noted under **Boyce/Codd normal form**, it's often more instructive with the normal forms to show a counterexample rather than an example per se. Consider, therefore, relvar SPJ, with attributes S# (supplier number), P# (part number), and J# (project number), and predicate "Supplier S# supplies part P# to project J#." Let that relvar be all key (i.e., subject to the key constraint KEY{S#,P#,J#}). Let it also be subject to the constraint that if (a) supplier Sx supplies part Py, and (b) part Py is supplied to project Jz, and (c) project Jz is supplied by supplier Sx, then (d) supplier Sx supplies part Py to project Jz. Then SPJ is equal to the join of its projections on {S#,P#}, {P#,J#}, and {J#,S#}—i.e., it satisfies the JD *{{S#,P#}, {P#,J#},{J#,S#}}—and so it can be nonloss decomposed into those three projections. Because that JD is neither trivial nor implied by the sole superkey (viz., the entire heading), relvar SPJ isn't in 5NF, though it is in 4NF.

first normal form Normalized. By definition, relvars are always in first normal form, 1NF (*see* **relation variable**). It follows that a "table" in a language such as SQL is in 1NF if and only if it's a direct and faithful representation of some relvar, where *direct and faithful* means, among other things, that every row-and-column intersection in that table contains exactly one value of the applicable type, nothing more and nothing less. (The value in question can be arbitrarily complex—it can even be a table—but, to repeat, there must be exactly one, and it must be of the applicable type.) In particular, therefore, a table isn't in first normal form if it includes any repeating groups, q.v. This fact accounts for the usual informal characterization of first normal form as meaning simply *no repeating groups. Note*: Although being in 1NF clearly doesn't preclude being in 2NF as well, the term *1NF* is often used loosely to refer to a relvar that's in 1NF only and not in any higher normal form.

first order logic A form of predicate logic in which the sets over which variables range are not allowed to contain predicates. *Contrast* **second order logic**. *Note*: Propositional logic, q.v., might be regarded as a "zeroth order" logic, because it has no variables (and its variables thus certainly don't range over anything at all).

flat relation The idea that "relations are flat" is a popular misconception. *See* **table**.

FORALL *See* **universal quantifier**. In the literature, FORALL is often represented by an upside-down A, thus: ∀.

foreign key Let $R1$ and $R2$ be relvars, not necessarily distinct, and let K be a key for $R1$. Let FK be a subset of the heading of $R2$ such that there exists a possibly empty sequence of attribute renamings that maps K into K' (say), where K' and FK contain exactly the same attributes. Then FK is a foreign key if and only if, at all times, every tuple in $R2$ is constrained to have an FK value that's the K' value for some (necessarily unique) tuple in $R1$ at the time in question. $R1$ and $R2$ here are the referenced relvar and the referencing relvar, respectively, and the constraint between them is a referential constraint.

Examples: In relvar SP, {S#} and {P#} are foreign keys corresponding to the keys {S#} and {P#} in relvars S and P, respectively. Note that the key in the referenced relvar that corresponds to a given foreign key is not required to be a primary key specifically.

foreign key constraint   A referential constraint.

foreign key rule   A rule to the effect that certain updates should trigger certain compensating actions, such as cascading a delete operation, with the aim of avoiding some referential integrity violation that might otherwise occur.

formal system   A logical system.

formula   Same as well-formed formula, q.v.

fourth normal form   Relvar R is in fourth normal form, 4NF, if and only if every nontrivial MVD satisfied by R is implied by some superkey of R. Every 4NF relvar is in BCNF. *Note*: 4NF is "the" normal form with respect to MVDs. Also, although being in 4NF clearly doesn't preclude being in the next higher normal form (5NF) as well, the term *4NF* is often used loosely to refer to a relvar that's in 4NF and not in 5NF. In any case, fourth normal form as such is no longer very important (BCNF, 5NF, and 6NF being the normal forms of most practical significance); we mention it here mainly for historical reasons.

Example: As noted under **Boyce/Codd normal form**, it's often more instructive with the normal forms to show a counterexample rather than an example per se. Consider, therefore, relvar CTX, with attributes C (course), T (teacher), and X (text), and predicate "Course C can be taught by teacher T and uses text X as a textbook." Let that relvar be all key (i.e., subject to the key constraint KEY{C,T,X}). Let it also be such that for a given course, the set of teachers and the set of texts are quite independent of each other. Then CTX is equal to the join of its projections on {C,T} and {C,X}—i.e., it satisfies the MVDs {C} →→ {T} and {C} →→ {X}—and so it can be nonloss decomposed into those two projections. Because those MVDs are neither trivial nor implied by the sole superkey (viz., the entire heading), relvar CTX isn't in 4NF, though it is in BCNF.

free variable In logic, a variable (more precisely, an occurrence within a predicate of a variable reference) that isn't bound—in other words, a parameter. (The term *variable* is used here in the sense of logic, not in the programming language sense.) *Contrast* **bound variable**.

Examples: Let the symbols x and y denote integers. Then the following expressions are both predicates, and x appears as a free variable in each of them:

```
x < 7
EXISTS y ( y > 3 ) AND x < 7
```

The first predicate is self-explanatory. The second is a little more complicated because it involves a quantified subexpression (in which y appears, twice, as a bound variable) as well as the free variable x.

Turning to a database example, the following is a query ("Get suppliers who supply at least one part") on the suppliers-and-parts database, expressed in tuple calculus:

```
S WHERE EXISTS SP ( SP.S# = S.S# )
```

The text following the keyword WHERE here is a predicate, and the reference to S in that predicate is free (by contrast, the references to SP are bound). Note, however, that in this particular example, the symbols S and SP denote not only variables in the sense of logic but also variables in the conventional programming language sense—but that's because we've indulged in a certain sleight of hand, as it were. Here's an extended version of the same example that should help to clarify matters:

```
SX  RANGES OVER { S }  ;
SPX RANGES OVER { SP } ;

SX WHERE EXISTS SPX ( SPX.S# = SX.S# )
```

Here, SX and SPX have been explicitly declared as variables in the sense of logic, ranging over (the current values of) relvars S and SP, respectively. Now it's the reference to SX that's free and the references to SPX that are bound. *Note*: Let *VR* be a variable reference that occurs prior to the WHERE clause in some tuple calculus expression. If *VR* also occurs in the predicate in that WHERE clause (which it often but not invariably will), then it must be free, not bound, in that boolean expression.

full FD Old-fashioned and somewhat deprecated term for a left-irreducible FD.

fully dependent Old-fashioned and somewhat deprecated term for irreducibly dependent.

fully normalized A database is fully normalized if and only if every relvar it contains is in at least 5NF (i.e., if and only if every such relvar is fully normalized in turn).

function *1. (Mathematics)* Given two sets (not necessarily distinct), a rule—also known as a mapping—pairing each element of the first set (the domain) with exactly one element of the second set (the codomain); equivalently, that pairing itself. The unique element y of the codomain corresponding to element x of the domain is the image of x (under the specified function), and the set of all such images is the range of that function. Note that the range is a subset (often a proper subset) of the codomain, and the function can be regarded as a directed relationship—in fact, a many-to-one correspondence, in the strict sense of that term—from the domain to the range. *2. (Programming languages)* A read-only operator (sometimes more specifically one denoted by an identifier such as SUM instead of a special symbol such as "+"). Note, however, that the programming language construct denoted by this term is precisely a function in the mathematical sense; thus, there's really only one concept here, not two. Note also that nothing in the definition requires the domain and codomain to be sets of scalars; thus, a read-only operator could be defined in terms of, say, three parameters, in which case the domain would consist of a set of triples (and similarly for the codomain).

Example: Let f be the rule that maps nonnegative integers x to their squares x^2. Then we can say that f is a function with (a) domain and codomain both the set of all nonnegative integers, and (b) range that subset of the codomain consisting only of perfect squares.

functional dependency Let *A* and *B* be subsets of the heading of relvar *R*. Then relvar *R* satisfies the functional dependency (FD) *A* → *B* if and only if, in every relation that's a legal value for *R*, whenever two tuples have the same value for *A*, they also have the same value for *B* (*A* here is called the determinant and *B* is called the dependent). *Note*: Functional dependency is also known as functional dependence. The FD *A* → *B* is read as "*B* is functionally dependent on *A*," or "*A* functionally determines *B*," or, more simply, just "*A* arrow *B*." Note too that *A* and *B* are, specifically, sets of attributes. Informally, however, it's common, though strictly incorrect, to speak of the attributes in *B* as if those attributes per se (instead of the set *B* that contains those attributes) were functionally dependent on *A*; likewise, it's common, though strictly incorrect, to speak of the attributes in *A* as if *B* were functionally dependent on those attributes per se (instead of on the set *A* that contains those attributes).

Example: Suppose for the sake of the example that relvar SP has an additional attribute CITY, representing the city of the applicable supplier. Then that revised version of SP satisfies the FD {S#} → {CITY}. Note in particular in this example that the determinant isn't a key of the relvar concerned. (By definition, every relvar *R* always satisfies all possible FDs of the form *K* → *X*, where *K* is a key—or, more generally, a superkey—for *R*, and *X* is an arbitrary subset of the heading of *R*. In other words, there are always "arrows out of superkeys," and it's "arrows not out of superkeys" that are, in a sense, the interesting ones.)

functionally dependent *See* functional dependency.

functionally determines *See* functional dependency.

generated type *See* type generator.

Golden Rule, The The rule that no database is ever allowed to violate its own total database constraint. It follows that no relvar is ever allowed to violate its own total relvar constraint either, a fortiori. (This latter, weaker requirement is often referred to as **The Golden Rule** as well, though strictly speaking it's merely a logical consequence of **The Golden Rule** proper.)

greater-than join A theta join in which theta is ">".

GROUP *See* grouping.

grouping Let *r* be a relation and let the heading of *r* be partitioned into subsets {*X*} and {*Y*}. Let the attributes of {*Y*} be $Y1, Y2, ..., Yn$; also, let {*X*} not contain any attribute called *YR*. Then the grouping *r* GROUP ({*Y*} AS *YR*) is another relation *s*. The heading of *s* consists of {*X*} extended with an attribute *YR* of type RELATION {*Y*}. The body of *s* is defined as follows: first, let *z* be the result of *r* WRAP ({*Y*} AS *YT*). Second, for each distinct *X* value *x* in *z*, (a) let *yr* be the relation whose tuples are all and only those *YT* values from tuples in *z* in which the *X* value is *x*; (b) let *t* be a tuple with *X* value *x* and *YR* value *yr* (and no other attributes); then, and only then, *t* is a tuple of *s*. *Note*: Given a relation *r* and some grouping of *r*, there's always an inverse ungrouping that will yield *r* again; however, the converse is not necessarily true. *See* **ungrouping**.

Example: The following expression denotes a grouping of the relation that's the current value of relvar SP:

```
SP GROUP ( { P#, QTY } AS PQ_REL )
```

That grouping is a relation *spq* of type RELATION {S# S#, PQ_REL RELATION {P# P#, QTY QTY}}. Relation *spq* contains one tuple for each distinct S# value currently appearing in relvar SP, and no other tuples. Given the sample values in Figure 1, for example, the *spq* tuple for supplier S2 has S# value S2 and a PQ_REL value that is a relation whose body contains just the tuples <P1,300> and <P2,400>.

hash An implementation construct.

heading A set of attributes, in which (by definition) each attribute is of the form <*A*,*T*>, where *A* is an attribute name and *T* is the type name for attribute *A*. Within any given heading, (a) distinct attributes are allowed to have the same type name but not the same attribute name; (b) the number of attributes is the degree (of the heading in question). Every subset of a heading is itself a heading. *Note*: Given that it's common to refer informally to an attribute by its attribute name alone, it's also common to regard a given heading informally as a set of attribute names alone.

Examples: The heading of relvar S is

```
{ <S#,S#>, <SNAME,NAME>, <STATUS,INTEGER>, <CITY,CHAR> }
```

The following (corresponding to a certain projection of relvar S) is also a heading:

```
{ <CITY,CHAR>, <SNAME,NAME> }
```

These two headings might be represented less formally as:

```
{ S#, SNAME, STATUS, CITY }
```

```
{ CITY, SNAME }
```

In **Tutorial D** they would be represented as follows:

```
{ S# S#, SNAME NAME, STATUS INTEGER, CITY CHAR }
```

```
{ CITY CHAR, SNAME NAME }
```

Heath's theorem   Let A, B, and C be subsets of the heading of relvar R, such that the set theory union of A, B, and C is equal to that heading. Let AB denote the set theory union of A and B, and similarly for AC. If R satisfies the FD $A \rightarrow B$, then R is equal to the join of its projections on AB and AC.

Example: Relvar S satisfies the FD {S#} $\rightarrow$ {SNAME,CITY}, so it's equal to the join of (and can be nonloss decomposed into) its projections on {S#,SNAME,CITY} and {S#,STATUS}.

host language   A programming language that relies on some data sublanguage (q.v.) for its database support. *Contrast* database programming language.

idempotent   Let Op be a dyadic operator, and assume for definiteness that Op is expressed in infix style. Then Op is idempotent if and only if, for all x, x Op $x = x$.

Examples: In logic, AND and OR are both idempotent, because

```
x AND x = x     and     x OR x = x
```

for all x. It follows as a direct consequence that JOIN and UNION, respectively, are idempotent in relational algebra.

identity   1. *(General)* That which distinguishes a given entity from all others. 2. *(Operator)* Equality. 3. *(Comparison)* A boolean expression of the form $(exp1) = (exp2)$, where $exp1$ and $exp2$ are expressions of the same type, that's guaranteed to evaluate to TRUE regardless of the values of any variables involved. The parentheses enclosing $exp1$ and $exp2$ might not be needed in practice. 4. *(Identity value)* Let *Op* be a commutative dyadic operator, and assume for definiteness that *Op* is expressed in infix style. If there exists a value *i* such that *i Op v* and *v Op i* are both equal to *v* for all possible argument values *v*, then *i* is the identity, or identity value, with respect to *Op*.

Examples (fourth definition only): The dyadic operators "+", "*", AND, OR, and JOIN have identity values 0, 1, TRUE, FALSE, and TABLE_DEE, respectively. Note the last of these in particular: it means, to spell the point out, that *r* JOIN TABLE_DEE = TABLE_DEE JOIN *r* = *r* for all possible relations *r*. It also means that, just as the sum of no numbers is zero (*see* **aggregate operator**), so the join of no relations is TABLE_DEE (*see* **natural join**).

identity projection   The projection of a given relation *r* over all of its attributes (i.e., *r*{*H*}, where {*H*} is the heading of *r*). Such a projection is guaranteed to be equal to *r*.

Example: The expression SP{S#,QTY,P#} is an identity projection.

identity restriction   A restriction of a given relation *r* that's equal to *r* (i.e., is equal to *r* WHERE TRUE); in particular, a restriction of the form *r* WHERE *t*, where *t* is a tautology (q.v.).

Examples: The expressions S WHERE STATUS ≠ 25 and S WHERE STATUS = STATUS are both identity restrictions (the second necessarily so, because STATUS = STATUS is a tautology).

identity value   *See* **identity**.

IF AND ONLY IF   Same as EQUIV.

IF ... THEN ...   Same as IMPLIES.

IFF   Same as EQUIV.

image   *See* **function**.

immediate checking   Checking an integrity constraint whenever an update is performed that might cause it to be violated. All constraint checking is immediate in the relational model. *Contrast* **deferred checking**.

immediate constraint   A constraint for which the checking is immediate (*see* **immediate checking**).

implementation A physical realization on a real machine of the abstract machine that constitutes some given data model (in the sense of the first definition of that term). In the interest of physical data independence, the model and its implementation should be kept rigidly apart; that is, the model should have nothing to say about any aspect of implementation.

implication If p and q are predicates, the implication (p) IMPLIES (q) is a predicate also. Let (pi) IMPLIES (qi) be an invocation of that predicate (where pi and qi are invocations of p and q, respectively). Then that invocation (pi) IMPLIES (qi) evaluates to TRUE if and only if pi evaluates to FALSE or qi evaluates to TRUE or both. (In other words, (p) IMPLIES (q) is equivalent to $(\text{NOT}(p))$ OR (q).) *Note*: The parentheses enclosing p and q in the expression (p) IMPLIES (q) might not be needed in practice.

implied by FDs Given a set s of FDs, a given FD is implied by s if and only if it's a logical consequence of the FDs in s according to Armstrong's inference rules, q.v.

implied by superkey(s) *See* FD implied by a superkey; JD implied by superkeys; MVD implied by a superkey.

IMPLIES *See* implication.

inclusion *See* set inclusion.

inclusion dependency A constraint to the effect that a given projection of a given relvar $R2$ is required to be equal at all times to some subset of a given projection of a given relvar $R1$ at the time in question ($R1$ and $R2$ are not necessarily distinct). Foreign key constraints are a special case.

IND An inclusion dependency.

independent projection *See* FD preservation.

index An implementation construct.

inference rule A rule for deriving a conclusion—a theorem—from a set of premises (i.e., other theorems, possibly axioms).

information equivalent Let $s1$ and $s2$ be sets of relations. Then $s1$ and $s2$ are information equivalent if and only if every relation in $s1$ is either identical to some relation in $s2$ or can be derived from the relations in $s2$ (*see* **derived relation**), and every relation in *s2* is either identical to some relation in *s1* or can be derived from the relations in *s1*.

Information Principle, The   The principle that the only kind of variable allowed in a relational database is the relation variable specifically. (Equivalently, a relational database contains relvars, and nothing but relvars.) *Note*: It has to be said that this principle isn't very well named. It might more accurately be called *The Principle of Uniform Representation*, or even *The Principle of Uniformity of Representation*, since the crucial point about it is that it implies that all information in a relational database is represented in one and only one way—namely, as relations.

inheritance   Type inheritance.

injection   A mapping, or function, from set *s1* to set *s2* such that each element of *s2* is the image of at most one element of *s1*. Also known as a nonloss, injective, or "one-to-one into" mapping (though *one-to-one* here isn't being used in its strict sense, q.v.).

Example: The mapping from nonnegative integers x to their squares x^2 is an injection from the set of all nonnegative integers to itself.

inner join   Join. The qualification *inner* is used to distinguish the join in question from its outer counterpart. (Outer join in turn has to do with nulls and three-valued logic and is therefore deliberately not discussed further in this dictionary.)

INSERT   Loosely, an operator that inserts a given set of tuples into a given relvar. It's shorthand for a certain relational assignment.

Example: The INSERT statement

```
INSERT SP
RELATION {
TUPLE { S# S#('S3'), P# P#('P1'), QTY QTY(150) },
TUPLE { S# S#('S5'), P# P#('P1'), QTY QTY(500) } } ;
```

is shorthand for the following relational assignment:

```
SP := ( SP ) UNION
      ( RELATION {
        TUPLE { S# S#('S3'), P# P#('P1'),
                              QTY QTY(150) },
        TUPLE { S# S#('S5'), P# P#('P1'),
                              QTY QTY(500) } } ) ;
```

In this example, the expressions S#('S3') and S#('S5') are selector invocations for type S#; the expression P#('P1') is a selector invocation for type P#; and the expressions QTY(150) and QTY(500) are selector invocations for type QTY. Likewise, the two expressions of the form TUPLE {...} are selector invocations for tuple type TUPLE {S# S#, P# P#, QTY QTY}, and the sole expression of the form RELATION {...} is a selector invocation for relation type RELATION {S# S#, P# P#, QTY QTY}. Note, incidentally, that with INSERT as defined here, it's not an error to try to insert a tuple that already exists in the target relvar. Replacing UNION in the expansion by D_UNION would solve this problem (if it is a problem).

instantiation An invocation of a predicate. *Note*: Actually, the logical notion of instantiation is more general than the familiar programming language notion of function invocation. Further details are beyond the scope of this dictionary.

integrity A database is in a state of integrity if and only if it violates no defined integrity constraints (i.e., if and only if it's consistent). Integrity is necessary but not sufficient for correctness. The relational model requires databases to be in a state of integrity at all times, where "at all times" really means at statement boundaries (except as noted under **type constraint**).

integrity constraint A named boolean expression that must be satisfied (i.e., is required to evaluate to TRUE) at all times, where "at all times" really means at statement boundaries (except as noted under **type constraint**). There are two basic kinds, database constraints and type constraints (q.v.). The DBMS should reject any update that, if accepted, would cause some integrity constraint to be violated (i.e., to evaluate to FALSE). *Note*: Because database constraints in particular affect updates, and updates apply by definition to variables specifically, it follows that such constraints apply to variables specifically too—i.e., anything thus constrained must be a variable, by definition.

intelligent key A single-attribute key that, in addition to its main purpose of identifying some entity, carries some kind of encoded information embedded within it. *Contrast* **surrogate key**.

Example: Let parts purchased from domestic suppliers be assigned part numbers in the range 0–4999, and parts purchased elsewhere be assigned part numbers in the range 5000–9999. Now assume the 5001st different kind of part is purchased from a domestic supplier. Clearly, the part numbering scheme will now have to be revised, and any application that previously relied on the fact that parts purchased domestically have numbers less than 5000 will therefore fail. As this example suggests, intelligent keys should be used with caution. (Actually, a similar remark applies to the encoding of information within any attribute, not just key attributes specifically, but key attributes seem to be particularly prone to this kind of abuse.)

intended interpretation   The informal, user-understood meaning (i.e., the relvar predicate, q.v.) for a given relvar. Also referred to as interpretation, unqualified.

intension   For a given relation or relvar, the intended interpretation, or sometimes the heading. *Contrast* **extension** (third definition).

Interchangeability Principle, The   *(Of base and virtual relvars)* The principle that there should be no arbitrary and unnecessary distinctions between base and virtual relvars; i.e., virtual relvars should "look and feel" just like base ones as far as users are concerned.

internal predicate   The total relvar constraint for a given relvar. The term is deprecated because it's at least arguably misleading (since relvar constraints are really propositions).

INTERSECT   *See* intersection.

intersection   1. *(Dyadic case)* The intersection of two relations *r1* and *r2*, *r1* INTERSECT *r2*, where *r1* and *r2* are of the same type *T*, is a relation of type *T* with body the set of all tuples *t* such that *t* appears in both *r1* and *r2*. 2. *(N-adic case)* The intersection of *n* relations *r1, r2, …, rn* ($n \geq 0$), INTERSECT {*r1,r2,…,rn*}, where *r1, r2, …, rn* are all of the same type *T*, is a relation of type *T*, with body the set of all tuples *t* such that *t* appears in each of *r1, r2, …, rn* (unless $n = 0$, in which case (a) some syntactic mechanism, not shown here, is needed to specify the pertinent type *T* and (b) the result is the universal relation, q.v., of that type). *Note*: The relational intersection operator is a special case of join, q.v.

Example: The expression (S{CITY}) INTERSECT (P{CITY}) denotes the intersection of the projections on CITY of the relations that are the current values of relvars S and P. That intersection is a relation of type RELATION {CITY CHAR}. Moreover, if the current values of relvars S and P are *s* and *p*, respectively, the body of that relation consists of all tuples of the form <*c*> that appear in both *s*{CITY} and *p*{CITY}— meaning *c* is a current supplier city that's also a current part city. Note that the expression (S{CITY}) INTERSECT (P{CITY}) is semantically equivalent to the expression (S{CITY}) JOIN (P{CITY}).

intersection (set theory)   The set of all elements appearing in both of two given sets. (This definition can obviously be extended to apply to any number of sets.)

irreducible   1. *(Of a key) See* **candidate key**. 2. *(Of a relvar)* Sixth normal form. 3. *(Of an FD)* Left-irreducible. 4. *(Of a set of FDs)* The set *s* of FDs is irreducible if and only if (a) the dependent in every FD in *s* contains only one attribute, (b) every FD in *s* is left-irreducible, and (c) no FD can be discarded from *s* without changing the closure of *s*.

irreducibly dependent   *(Of a dependent in an FD)* Let *A* and *B* be subsets of the heading of some relvar *R*. Then *B* is irreducibly dependent on *A* if and only if it's functionally dependent on *A* and not on any proper subset of *A*.

Example: In relvar SP, {QTY} is irreducibly dependent on {S#,P#}. It's also dependent on {S#,P#,QTY}, but not irreducibly so.

irreducibly equivalent   *(Of a set of FDs)* Let *s1* and *s2* be sets of FDs. Then *s1* is an irreducible equivalent of *s2* if it's equivalent to *s2* and irreducible.

IS_EMPTY   A **Tutorial D** operator that returns TRUE or FALSE according as a specified relation is empty or not.

isomorphism   Let *s1* and *s2* be sets (not necessarily distinct), and let *f* be a bijective mapping from *s1* to *s2*. Let *OpX* be an operator that takes elements of *s1* as its operands and yields an element of *s1* as its result. Then *f* is an isomorphism if and only if, for all such operators *OpX*, there exists an analogous operator

OpY that takes elements of *s2* as its operands and yields an element of *s2* as its result such that, whenever *OpX* applied to *x1*, *x2*, ..., *xn* yields *x*, then *OpY* applied to *y1*, *y2*, ..., *yn* yields *y*, where *y1*, *y2*, ..., *yn*, and *y* are the images of *x1*, *x2*, ..., *xn*, and *x*, respectively, under *f*. In other words, a bijective mapping is an isomorphism if and only if it preserves the algebraic structure of the domain *s1* in the codomain *s2*. *Note*: If the bijective mapping *f* is an isomorphism, then its inverse is an isomorphism as well.

Example: Let *s1* be the set {EVEN,ODD} and let operators "+" and "*" be defined as follows:

+	EVEN	ODD
EVEN	EVEN	ODD
ODD	ODD	EVEN

*	EVEN	ODD
EVEN	EVEN	EVEN
ODD	EVEN	ODD

Now let *s2* be the set {TRUE,FALSE} and let *f* be a bijection from *s1* to *s2* that maps EVEN and ODD to TRUE and FALSE, respectively. Further, let the logical operators EQUIV and OR correspond to "+" and "*", respectively. Then *f* is an isomorphism from *s1* (with its operators "+" and "*") to *s2* (with its operators EQUIV and OR).

JD Join dependency.

JD implied by superkeys The JD *{*A1,A2,...,An*} is implied by superkeys if and only if each of *A1*, *A2*, ..., *An* is a superkey for the pertinent relvar *R*.

JOIN *See* natural join.

join Natural join (unless the context demands otherwise).

join dependency A generalization of the concept of multivalued dependency (every MVD is a JD, but some JDs aren't MVDs). Let *A1*, *A2*, ..., *An* be subsets of the heading of relvar *R*. Then *R* satisfies the join dependency (JD) *{*A1,A2,...,An*} if and only if every relation that's a legal value for *R* is equal to the join of its projections on *A1*, *A2*, ..., *An*. *Note*: The JD *{*A1,A2,...,An*} is read as "star *A1*, *A2*, ..., *An*."

Example: Relvar S satisfies the JD

```
* { { S#, SNAME }, { S#, STATUS }, { S#, CITY } }
```

because every relation that's a legal value for S is equal to the join of its projections on {S#,SNAME}, {S#,STATUS}, and {S#,CITY}; i.e., relvar S could be nonloss decomposed into those three projections. (Of course, there's no requirement that this decomposition actually be performed—whether it should or not depends on whether there's any advantage to be gained by doing so.)

key A candidate key (unless the context demands otherwise).

key constraint A constraint to the effect that a given subset of the heading of a given relvar is a candidate key for that relvar.

left-irreducible FD Given a set *s* of FDs, the FD *f* in *s* is left-irreducible (with respect to *s*) if and only if no attribute can be discarded from the determinant of *f* without changing the closure of *s*.

Examples: Let *s* be the set of all FDs satisfied by relvar SP. Then the FDs {S#,P#} → {QTY} and {S#,P#,QTY} → {QTY} both appear in *s*. Of these two FDs, the first is left-irreducible but the second isn't.

less-than join A theta join in which theta is "<".

literal 1. *(Programming languages)* Loosely, a self-defining symbol; a symbol that denotes a value that can be determined at compile time. More precisely, a literal is a symbol that denotes a value that's fixed and determined by the symbol in question (and the type of that value is therefore also fixed and determined by the symbol in question). Every value of every type, tuple and relation types included, must be denotable by means of some literal. *Note*: A literal is a special case of a selector invocation (*see* **selector**). 2. *(Logic)* A simple proposition or its negation; a simple predicate or its negation (*see* **simple predicate**; **simple proposition**).

Examples (first definition only): 4 (a literal of type INTEGER); 'ABC' (a literal of type CHAR); FALSE (a literal of type BOOLEAN); S#('S1') (a literal of type S#); TUPLE {S# S#('S1'), P# P#('P1'), QTY QTY(300)} (a literal of type TUPLE {S# S#, P# P#, QTY QTY}); RELATION {TUPLE {S# S#('S1'), P# P#('P1'), QTY QTY(300)}} (a literal of type RELATION {S# S#, P# P#, QTY QTY}); and so on.

logic The scientific study of the methods and principles used in valid reasoning.

logic variable A variable that can appear either bound or free in predicate calculus expressions. *See also* range variable.

logical data independence *See* data independence.

logical database design The process (or the result of the process) of deciding, given some body of data to be represented in some database, what relvars that database should contain, what attributes they should have, and what constraints they should be subject to. Ideally, the goal is to produce a design that's independent of all considerations having to do with either physical implementation or specific applications—the latter objective being desirable for the good reason that it's generally not the case that all uses to which the database will be put are known at design time. Overall, the design process can be summarized as one of (a) pinning down the relvar predicates (or "business rules") as carefully as possible, albeit necessarily somewhat informally, and then (b) mapping those relvar predicates to specific relvars and formal constraints.

logical expression A boolean expression.

logical implication Implication.

logical operator An operator that (a) takes either values or variables (or both) of type BOOLEAN as operands, and (b) either returns a value, or updates at least one variable, of type BOOLEAN. The connectives are a special case.

logical system Loosely, a system consisting of axioms and inference rules, together with a set of theorems that can be derived from the former by means of the latter. More precisely, a logical system consists of (a) a set of symbols (e.g., NOT, AND, punctuation symbols, variable names); (b) a set of grammatical rules for forming sentences within the system; (c) a set of given sentences (the axioms); and (d) a set of rules for inferring "new" sentences from "old" ones (the rules of inference).

Examples: Propositional logic and predicate logic are both logical systems.

lossless decomposition Nonloss decomposition.

lossy decomposition   A decomposition that isn't nonloss.

> *Example*: The decomposition of relvar S into its projections on {S#,SNAME} and {SNAME,STATUS,CITY} is lossy because it isn't guaranteed that, at all times, S is equal to the join of those projections.

many-to-many correspondence   Strictly, a rule pairing two sets *s1* and *s2* (*s1* and *s2* not necessarily distinct) such that each element of *s1* corresponds to at least one element of *s2* and each element of *s2* corresponds to at least one element of *s1*; equivalently, that pairing itself. Often used loosely, however, to mean a pairing such that either (a) each element of *s1* corresponds to any number of elements of *s2* (possibly none at all) and each element of *s2* corresponds to at least one element of *s1*, or (b) each element of *s1* corresponds to at least one element of *s2* and each element of *s2* corresponds to any number of elements of *s1* (possibly none at all), or (c) each element of *s1* corresponds to any number of elements of *s2* (possibly none at all) and each element of *s2* corresponds to any number of elements of *s1* (possibly none at all). The term is best avoided unless the intended meaning is clear.

> *Example (strict sense only):* Let *s* be the set of all positive integers. Consider the pairing of positive integers *x* and *y* defined as follows: positive integers *x* and *y* are paired if and only if they have the same number of digits in conventional decimal notation. Then that pairing is a many-to-many correspondence from *s* to itself.

many-to-one correspondence   Strictly, a rule pairing two sets *s1* and *s2* (*s1* and *s2* not necessarily distinct) such that each element of *s1* corresponds to exactly one element of *s2* and each element of *s2* corresponds to at least one element of *s1* (in other words, a surjection, q.v.); equivalently, that pairing itself. Often used loosely, however, to mean a pairing such that (a) each element of *s1* corresponds to at most one element of *s2* and each element of *s2* corresponds to at least one element of *s1*, or (b) each element of *s1* corresponds to exactly one element of *s2* and each element of *s2* corresponds to any number of elements of *s1* (possibly none at all), or (c) each element of *s1* corresponds to at most one element of *s2* and each element of *s2* corresponds to any number of elements of *s1* (possibly none at all). The term is best avoided unless the intended meaning is clear.

Example (strict sense only): Let *s1* and *s2* be the set of all integers and the set of all nonnegative integers, respectively. Then the pairing of integers *x* with their absolute values |*x*| is a many-to-one correspondence from *s1* to *s2*.

mapping   A function.

mark   *See* null.

MATCHING   *See* semijoin.

material implication   Implication.

materialization   A somewhat unsophisticated technique for implementing operations on views according to which (a) the relational expression that defines the view is evaluated at the time the operation is invoked, (b) the view is thereby materialized, and (c) the operation in question is then executed against the relation so materialized. Note that this technique can't be used for implementing view updates but is limited to read-only operations. *Contrast* materialized view; substitution (first definition).

materialized view   Deprecated term for a snapshot. Note the difference between (a) materialization as a technique for implementing operations on views and (b) a "materialized view" (i. e., a snapshot) as such. The former is an implementation technique and should have no logical consequences for the user at all (i.e., users shouldn't need to know whether a given operation on a given view is implemented by materialization). By contrast, the latter is an issue that concerns the user very much; i.e., the user certainly does need to know whether a given relvar is a snapshot, because whether it is or not affects the semantics of the relvar in question. The problem is, however, that (as the definition indicates) snapshots have come to be known, at least in some circles, not as snapshots at all but as materialized views. But snapshots aren't views; views are virtual and snapshots aren't, and "materialized view" is a contradiction in terms (at least as far as the model is concerned). Worse yet, the unqualified term *view* is often taken to mean a materialized view specifically, and thus we're in danger of no longer having a good term for a view in the original sense. This dictionary does use *view* in its original sense, but be warned that the term doesn't always have that meaning elsewhere. *Caveat lector.*

meaning *(Of a relvar)* *See* relvar constraint (second definition); relvar predicate.

member An element of a bag or set.

merge A join implementation technique.

metadata Data about data. *See* catalog.

minimality *(Of a key or of a set of FDs)* Old-fashioned and somewhat deprecated term for irreducibility.

MINUS *See* difference.

missing information A term often used to refer to information that's either currently unknown or inapplicable. *Note:* To say that information that's currently unknown is missing is possibly reasonable. However, to say that information that's inapplicable is missing isn't reasonable at all (and the usage is therefore deprecated). For example, if a given employee is unmarried, spouse information for that employee isn't missing; rather, it simply doesn't exist.

model Either a data model in general (usually in the sense of the first definition of that term) or the relational model specifically, as the context demands. *Note:* Actually, the term *model* has been given a great number of additional meanings in the literature—in fact, more meanings than it can reasonably be expected to bear. Such additional meanings are deliberately omitted here.

monadic *(Of an operator)* Having exactly one operand; i.e., being defined in terms of exactly one parameter.

multi-relvar constraint Informally, an integrity constraint that mentions two or more distinct relvars. *Contrast* single-relvar constraint. *Note:* The difference between single- and multi-relvar constraints is more a matter of pragma than logic, thanks to *The Principle of Interchangeability*.

Examples: The foreign key constraints from relvar SP to relvars S and P; also constraint C3 from the examples under database constraint.

multidependent *See* multivalued dependency.

multidetermines *See* multivalued dependency.

multiple assignment An operation that allows several individual assignments all to be performed "simultaneously," without any integrity checking being done until all of the individual assignments have been executed in their entirety.

Example: The following "double DELETE" is, logically, a multiple assignment operation:

```
DELETE S  WHERE S# = S#('S1') ,
DELETE SP WHERE S# = S#('S1') ;
```

Note the comma separator after the first DELETE, which indicates syntactically that the end of the overall statement has not yet been reached.

multiset A bag.

multivalued dependency A generalization of the concept of functional dependency (every FD is an MVD, but some MVDs aren't FDs). Let A, B, and C be subsets of the heading of relvar R such that the set theory union of A, B, and C is equal to that heading. Let AB denote the set theory union of A and B, and similarly for AC. Then R satisfies the multivalued dependencies (MVDs) $A \rightarrow\rightarrow B$ and $A \rightarrow\rightarrow C$ if and only if R satisfies the JD *{AB,AC}. *Note:* Multivalued dependency is also known as multivalued dependence. The MVD $A \rightarrow\rightarrow B$ is read as "B is multidependent on A," or "A multidetermines B," or, more simply, "A double arrow B." Note that A and B here are, specifically, *sets* of attributes. Informally, however, it's common, though strictly incorrect, to speak of the attributes in B as if those attributes per se (instead of the set B that contains those attributes) were multidependent on A; likewise, it's common, though strictly incorrect, to speak of the attributes in A as if B were multidependent on those attributes per se (instead of on the set A that contains those attributes). Observe that if relvar R satisfies the MVDs $A \rightarrow\rightarrow B$ and $A \rightarrow\rightarrow C$, then if it contains the tuples <a,b1,c1> and <a,b2,c2>, it also contains the tuples <a,b1,c2> and <a,b2,c1>. Observe further that it's apparent from the definition that relvar R can be nonloss decomposed into its projections on AB and AC if and only if it satisfies the MVDs $A \rightarrow\rightarrow B$ and $A \rightarrow\rightarrow C$ (this theorem, a stronger form of Heath's theorem, is one of many due to Fagin).

mutator Term sometimes used (especially in OO contexts) for an update operator.

MVD   Multivalued dependency.

MVD implied by a superkey   The MVD $A \rightarrow\rightarrow B$ is implied by a superkey if and only if A is a superkey for the pertinent relvar.

n-adic   *(Of an operator)* Having exactly n operands; i.e., being defined in terms of exactly n parameters ($n \geq 0$).

n-ary   Of degree n ($n \geq 0$).

n-place   *(Of a predicate)* n-adic ($n \geq 0$).

n-tuple   A tuple of degree n ($n \geq 0$).

NAND   In logic, a dyadic connective (also known as the *Sheffer stroke* and usually written as a vertical bar, "|"); if p and q are predicates, then $(p)|(q)$ is a predicate also. Let $(pi)|(qi)$ be an invocation of that predicate (where pi and qi are invocations of p and q, respectively). Then that invocation $(pi)|(qi)$ evaluates to FALSE if and only if pi and qi both evaluate to TRUE. (In other words, $(p)|(q)$ is equivalent to NOT$((p)$ AND $(q))$.) *Note:* The parentheses enclosing p and q in the expression $(p)|(q)$ might not be needed in practice.

natural join   1. *(Dyadic case)* Let relations $r1$ and $r2$ be such that attributes with the same name are of the same type. Then the natural join of $r1$ and $r2$, $r1$ JOIN $r2$, is a relation with heading the set theory union of the headings of $r1$ and $r2$ and with body the set of all tuples t such that t is the set theory union of a tuple from $r1$ and a tuple from $r2$. 2. *(N-adic case)* Let relations $r1, r2, \ldots, rn$ ($n \geq 0$) be such that attributes with the same name are of the same type. Then the natural join JOIN $\{r1,r2,\ldots,rn\}$ is defined as follows: if $n = 0$, the result is TABLE_DEE; if $n = 1$, the result is $r1$; otherwise, choose any two relations from the set $r1, r2, \ldots, rn$ and replace them by their (dyadic) natural join and repeat this process until the set consists of only one relation r, which is the overall result.

Example: The expression S JOIN SP denotes the natural join of the relations that are the current values of relvars S and SP. That join is a relation of type RELATION {S# S#, SNAME NAME, STATUS INTEGER, CITY CHAR, P# P#, QTY QTY}. Moreover, if the current values of relvars S and SP are *s* and *sp*, respectively, the body of that relation consists of all tuples of the form <s#,n,st,c,p#,q> such that the tuple <s#,n,st,c> appears in *s* and the tuple <s#,p#,q> appears in *sp*.

negation If *p* is a predicate, its negation NOT(*p*) is a predicate also. Let NOT(*pi*) be an invocation of that predicate (where *pi* is an invocation of *p*). Then that invocation NOT(*pi*) evaluates to TRUE if and only if *pi* evaluates to FALSE. *Note:* The parentheses enclosing *p* in the expression NOT(*p*) might not be needed in practice.

nested relation *See* relation-valued attribute.

NF² NF squared; short for NFNF ("non first normal form"). An NF² relvar is, loosely, a relvar with at least one relation-valued attribute. The term is deprecated, however, because it's based on a flawed understanding of the concept of first normal form. Also, the NF² concept is usually taken to include certain extensions to the conventional relational operators, extensions that aren't simply shorthand and thus aren't included (or needed) in the relational model.

niladic *(Of an operator)* Having no operands; i.e., being defined in terms of no parameters. *Note:* An operator might appear to be niladic syntactically and yet not be limited to having the same effect on every invocation, owing to its use of what might be called hidden arguments (such as the system clock). Indeed, niladic operators with such hidden arguments are the normal case.

Example: Many languages provide a built-in operator for generating random (or "pseudorandom") numbers. Such operators effectively have a hidden argument—viz., the random number returned on the previous invocation.

nonloss decomposition Replacing a relvar *R* by its projections *R1, R2, ..., Rn,* such that (a) the join of *R1, R2, ..., Rn* is guaranteed to be equal to *R,* and usually also such that (b) each of *R1, R2, ..., Rn* is needed in order to provide that guarantee (i.e., none of those projections is redundant in the join). Note that one "nonloss decomposition" that's always available for any given relvar *R* is to "replace" *R* by the corresponding identity projection (q.v.).

Example: A nonloss decomposition that might be applied to the suppliers-and-parts database would be to replace relvar S by its projections on {S#,SNAME} and {S#,STATUS,CITY}. Relvar S could then be obtained by joining those two projections back together again.

nonscalar Not scalar. The most important nonscalar constructs in the relational model are tuples and (especially) relations themselves.

nontrivial *(Of an FD, JD, or MVD)* Not trivial. *See* trivial FD; trivial JD; trivial MVD.

NOR In logic, a dyadic connective (also known as the *Peirce arrow* and usually written as a down arrow, "$\downarrow$"); if p and q are predicates, then $(p)\downarrow(q)$ is a predicate also. Let $(pi)\downarrow(qi)$ be an invocation of that predicate (where pi and qi are invocations of p and q, respectively). Then that invocation $(pi)\downarrow(qi)$ evaluates to TRUE if and only if pi and qi both evaluate to FALSE. (In other words, $(p)\downarrow(q)$ is equivalent to NOT$((p)$ OR $(q))$.) *Note:* The parentheses enclosing p and q in the expression $(p)\downarrow(q)$ might not be needed in practice.

normal form 1. Canonical form. 2. *See* first normal form; second normal form; etc. *Note:* The most important relational normal forms are BCNF and 5NF (and 6NF); the others are of mainly historical interest.

normalization The process of using the principles of nonloss decomposition to replace some given relvar by certain of its projections, such that the join of those projections is guaranteed to be equal to the original relvar. Note, therefore, that projection is the decomposition operator, and join the recomposition operator, with respect to the normalization process (as this latter term is usually understood). The objective of normalization is to reduce redundancy (q.v.) and thereby to eliminate certain update anomalies (q.v.) that might otherwise occur.

normalized relvar A relvar. (Relvars are always normalized by definition, in the sense that they're in at least first normal form. However, the term *normalized* is frequently, though somewhat inaccurately, used to refer to some normal form higher than first—especially either BCNF or 5NF.)

NOT *See* negation.

NOT MATCHING *See* semidifference.

null A construct, used in SQL in particular, for representing missing information (q.v.). *Note:* By definition, nulls aren't values (they're sometimes said to be *marks*); it follows that a "type" that "contains a null" isn't a type, a "tuple" that "contains a null" isn't a tuple, and a "relation" that "contains a null" isn't a relation. It follows further that nulls have no place in the relational model, and this dictionary therefore has very little to say regarding most null-related concepts.

nullary Of degree zero. The term is probably best avoided because of the potential confusion with null, q.v.

nullary foreign key A foreign key of degree zero.

nullary heading The heading of degree zero.

nullary key A key of degree zero.

nullary projection The projection of a given relation r over no attributes (i.e., $r\{\}$). The result is TABLE_DUM if r is empty and TABLE_DEE otherwise.

nullary relation A relation of degree zero. There are exactly two such, TABLE_DEE and TABLE_DUM.

nullary tuple The empty tuple; i.e., the tuple of degree zero.

nullology The study of the empty set. The term has nothing to do with null, q.v.

object A thing.

object ID A pointer.

object oriented / object orientation Leaning toward things.

object/relational database A relational database (*see* object/relational DBMS).

object/relational DBMS A relational DBMS. *Note:* In practice, the major distinction between commercial DBMSs that claim to provide object/relational support and those that don't is simply that the former allow users to define their own types. But a true relational DBMS does so too, and a DBMS that doesn't provide such support can hardly claim to be fully relational, even if it supports other aspects of the relational model. The fact is, the term *object/relational* is little more than a marketing label, dreamt up to conceal the fact that early "relational" products weren't very relational at all. Hence the present definition, to the effect that "object/relational" simply means *relational*.

observer Term sometimes used (especially in OO contexts) for a read-only operator.

one-to-many correspondence Strictly, a rule pairing two sets *s1* and *s2* (*s1* and *s2* not necessarily distinct) such that each element of *s1* corresponds to at least one element of *s2* and each element of *s2* corresponds to exactly one element of *s1*; equivalently, that pairing itself. Often used loosely, however, to mean a pairing such that either (a) each element of *s1* corresponds to any number of elements of *s2* (possibly none at all) and each element of *s2* corresponds to exactly one element of *s1*, or (b) each element of *s1* corresponds to at least one element of *s2* and each element of *s2* corresponds to at most one element of *s1*, or (c) each element of *s1* corresponds to any number of elements of *s2* (possibly none at all) and each element of *s2* corresponds to at most one element of *s1*. The term is best avoided unless the intended meaning is clear.

Example (strict sense only): Let *s1* and *s2* be the set of all nonnegative numbers and the set of all numbers, respectively. Then the pairing of nonnegative numbers x with their square roots $\pm\sqrt{x}$ is a one-to-many correspondence from *s1* to *s2*.

one-to-one correspondence Strictly, a rule pairing two sets *s1* and *s2* (*s1* and *s2* not necessarily distinct) such that each element of *s1* corresponds to exactly one element of *s2* and each element of *s2* corresponds to exactly one element of *s1* (in other words, a bijection, q.v.); equivalently, that pairing itself. Often used loosely, however, to mean a pairing such that (a) each element of *s1* corresponds to at most one element of *s2* and each element of *s2* corresponds to exactly one element of *s1*, or (b) each element of *s1* corresponds to exactly one element of *s2* and each element of *s2* corresponds to at most one element of *s1*, or (c) each element of *s1* corresponds to at most one element of *s2* and each element of *s2* corresponds to at most one element of *s1*. The term is best avoided unless the intended meaning is clear.

Example (strict sense only): Let *s* be the set of all integers. Then the pairing of elements x with their successors $x+1$ is a one-to-one correspondence from *s* to itself; so is the pairing of elements x with their predecessors $x-1$.

OO Object-oriented or object orientation, as the context demands.

open WFF A WFF that isn't closed; i.e., a WFF that denotes a predicate that isn't a proposition.

Open World Assumption, The The assumption—usually rejected in favor of The Closed World Assumption, q.v.—that (a) if a given tuple appears in a given relvar at a given time, then the proposition represented by that tuple is true at that time, and (b) if a given tuple could appear in that relvar at that time but doesn't, then the proposition represented by that tuple might or might not be true at that time.

operation An operator; sometimes, the process performed when an operator is invoked.

operator Either a read-only operator or an update operator. *Note*: The term is often used more specifically to mean a read-only operator that's denoted by some special symbol such as "+" instead of an identifier such as SUM, in which case other read-only operators (i.e., those denoted by identifiers) are typically referred to as functions.

optimizer The part of the DBMS responsible for mapping user requests (i.e., queries and updates) to the "best possible" executable code, where "best possible" basically means *best performing*.

OR *See* disjunction.

ordering The process, or the result of the process, of imposing a left-to-right sequence on the attributes—and, more especially, a top-to-bottom sequence on the tuples—of a relation, so that the data in the relation in question can be transferred out of the relational context and into an environment that relies on such orderings. Operators that request such orderings are of major pragmatic importance, but they aren't relational operators because their result isn't a relation.

Example: The SQL operators that provide this functionality are SELECT (for left-to-right column sequence) and ORDER BY (for top-to-bottom row sequence).

ordinal type A type with the property that the operator ">" is defined for every pair of values of the type in question. If $v1$ and $v2$ are two such values and are distinct, then exactly one of the expressions $v1 > v2$ and $v2 > v1$ evaluates to TRUE and the other to FALSE. Note that, since the "=" operator applies to values of every type, and given also the availability of the NOT connective, it follows that all of the usual comparison operators—"=", "≠", ">", "≥", "<", and "≤"—are available for all pairs of values of an ordinal type.

Examples: Type INTEGER is an ordinal type. By contrast, suppose the system also supports a type POINT, perhaps user-defined, representing geometric points in two-dimensional space. Then type POINT wouldn't be an ordinal type, because the notion of one point being somehow greater than another makes no sense.

orthogonal Independent.

orthogonal decomposition A decomposition of some given relvar into restrictions, such that the restrictions in question satisfy *The Principle of Orthogonal Design*.

Examples: Suppose we were to replace relvar P by two relvars LP and HP, LP containing tuples for parts with weight less than or equal to 17.0 and HP containing tuples for parts with weight greater than 17.0; then that decomposition would be orthogonal. By contrast, suppose relvar HP were defined to contain tuples for parts with weight greater than *or equal to* 17.0; then the decomposition wouldn't be orthogonal, because tuples for parts with weight equal to 17.0 would logically belong to both LP and HP.

Orthogonal Design Principle, The Loosely, the principle that no two relvars in a given database should have overlapping meanings. More precisely, let A and B be distinct relvars. Replace A and B by nonloss decompositions into projections $A1, A2, \ldots, Am$ and $B1, B2, \ldots, Bn$, respectively, such that every Ai ($i = 1, 2, \ldots, m$) and every Bj ($j = 1, 2, \ldots, n$) is in 6NF. Let some i and j be such that there exists a sequence of zero or more attribute renamings with the property that (a) when applied to Ai, it produces Ak, and (b) Ak and Bj are of the same type. Then there must not exist a constraint to the effect that, at all times, $Ak' = Bj'$ (where Ak' and Bj' are specified restrictions of Ak and Bj—say Ak WHERE a and Bj WHERE b, respectively—such that neither a nor b is a contradiction, q.v.).

overloading Using the same name for two or more different operators. The operators in question should preferably have similar semantics. *Note:* Overloading is also referred to more specifically as overloading polymorphism; it's also known as ad hoc polymorphism. In an inheritance context, the term is also sometimes used to refer to what is much better called inclusion polymorphism; this particular usage is deprecated, however, because it's based on a flawed perception of the nature of subtypes and supertypes. Further details are beyond the scope of this dictionary.

Examples: UNION is overloaded, because it (i.e., the name) is used for both relational and tuple union. Likewise, "=" is overloaded, because it applies to values of every type (i.e., there's an "=" operator for integers, another for supplier numbers, another for relations of type RELATION {S# S#, P# P#, QTY QTY}, and so on).

OWA The Open World Assumption.

parameter A formal operand in terms of which some operator is defined, to be replaced by some argument when the operator in question is invoked. Every parameter is declared to be of some type; any argument corresponding to a given parameter must be of the same type as that parameter.

Peirce arrow *See* NOR.

persistence The property according to which data, once inserted into the database, remains there ("persists") until explicitly deleted.

physical data independence *See* data independence.

physical database design The process (or the result of the process) of deciding, given some logical database design, how that logical design should map to whatever physical structures the target DBMS happens to support. Note, therefore, that the physical design should be derived from the logical design and not the other way around.

PJ/NF Projection-join normal form.

placeholder A free variable or parameter.

pointer An implementation construct. As is well known, pointers are excluded from the relational model. In fact, mixing pointers and relations—that is, allowing a "relation" to have an "attribute" whose values are pointers to "tuples" in some other "relation" (a state of affairs supported by several SQL products as well as by the SQL standard, despite the fact that it violates, among other things, *The Information Principle*)—has been described as **The Second Great Blunder**. (For the first, *see* **type**.) *See also* **referencing**.

polymorphism Loosely, the idea that an operator might permit its arguments to be of different types on different invocations. *See* **overloading**.

power set The set of all subsets of a given set. If the given set has cardinality n, the power set has cardinality 2^n.

predicate A truth-valued function. If and only if the corresponding set of parameters is empty, the predicate is a proposition.

predicate calculus A sound and complete formal system having to do with predicates and connectives and the inferences that can be made using them. *Note:* The principal difference between predicate calculus and propositional calculus, q.v., is that predicates, unlike propositions, are allowed to contain variables and quantifiers, which makes predicate calculus more powerful and more widely applicable.

predicate logic Predicate calculus.

prenex normal form A predicate is in prenex normal form if and only if all of the quantifiers appear at the beginning.

Example: Consider the following tuple calculus query ("Get suppliers who supply at least one red part"):

```
SX  RANGES OVER { S }  ;
SPX RANGES OVER { SP } ;
PX  RANGES OVER { P }  ;

SX WHERE
EXISTS PX ( PX.COLOR = 'Red' AND
            EXISTS SPX ( SPX.S# = SX.S# AND
                         SPX.P# = PX.P# ) )
```

The predicate in the WHERE clause here is not in prenex normal form. Here, however, is a semantically equivalent formulation of the query in which the predicate is in prenex normal form:

```
SX WHERE
EXISTS PX ( EXISTS SPX ( PX.COLOR = 'Red' AND
                         SPX.S# = SX.S# AND
                         SPX.P# = PX.P# ) )
```

primary key A candidate key that has been singled out for special syntactic treatment for some reason. While a given relvar can have any number of candidate keys, it can have at most one primary key. For a given relvar, however, whether some candidate key is to be chosen as primary, and if so, which one, are essentially psychological issues, outside the purview of the relational model. *Note:* The relational model originally insisted that base relvars, at least, should always have a primary key. It also insisted that foreign keys refer to primary keys specifically. However, there were never any good logical reasons for these rules, and rules that apply to base relvars but not to other kinds are more than a little suspect in any case (because they violate *The Principle of Interchangeability*); thus, the primary key notion could be dropped without serious loss. We mention it here mainly for historical reasons.

primitive operator Loosely, an operator not defined in terms of others. More precisely, let *s* be a set of operators. Let *Op* be an operator in *s* that can be defined in terms of other operators in *s*; remove *Op* from *s*, and repeat this step until it can't be repeated anymore. What remains is a set of operators that are primitive with respect to *s*. Note that the set of primitive operators with respect to a given set *s* is not necessarily unique.

Example: For relational algebra, a primitive set of operators will definitely include projection and almost certainly join, but not semijoin (because semijoin can be defined in terms of projection and join).

Principle of Identity of Indiscernibles, The The principle that if there's no way whatsoever of distinguishing between two objects, then there aren't two objects but only one. Or, equivalently: every object has its own unique identity. *Note:* In the relational model, such identities are represented in the same way as everything else—namely, by means of attribute values (*see Information Principle, The*)—and numerous benefits accrue from this fact. Note too that there's a logical difference between indiscernibility and interchangeability—two objects might be interchangeable and yet distinguishable (think of two pennies, for example). Note finally that the term *object* here is not being used in its object-oriented sense.

Principle of Interchangeability, The   *See Interchangeability Principle, The.*

Principle of Orthogonal Design, The   *See Orthogonal Design Principle, The.*

product   Cartesian product (unless the context demands otherwise).

projection   Let *r* be a relation and let {*X*} be a subset of the heading of *r*. Then the projection *r*{*X*} is a relation with heading {*X*} and body consisting of all tuples *x* such that there exists some tuple *t* in *r* with *X* value *x*. *See also* **tuple projection**.

Example: The expression S{STATUS,CITY} denotes a projection of the relation that's the current value of relvar S. That projection is a relation of type RELATION {STATUS INTEGER, CITY CHAR}, containing all possible tuples of the form <*st,c*> (and no other tuples) such that there exists some supplier number *s#* and some name *n* such that the tuple <*s#,n,st,c*> appears in the current value of relvar S. Given the sample values of Figure 1, the result has cardinality four. *Note:* For reasons of user friendliness, **Tutorial D** allows projections to be expressed in terms of the attributes to be discarded instead of those to be retained; thus, for example, the projection S{STATUS,CITY} can equivalently be expressed as S{ALL BUT S#,SNAME}. A similar remark applies to several other relational (and tuple) operations also.

projection-join normal form   Fifth normal form. The alternative (and original) name derives from the fact that 5NF is "the" normal form with respect to projection and join (as those operators are classically understood).

proper inclusion   Set *s2* is properly included in set *s1* if and only if it is a proper subset of *s1*.

proper subset   Set *s2* is a proper subset of set *s1* if and only if it is a subset of *s1* and *s1* and *s2* are distinct.

proper superkey A superkey that does not have the irreducibility property; i.e., a proper superset of a key.

proper superset Set *s1* is a proper superset of set *s2* if and only if it is a superset of *s2* and *s1* and *s2* are distinct.

property A thing belonging to another thing. *Note:* It's frequently suggested that there should be a one-to-one correspondence between "properties of interest" and attributes in base relvars. The suggestion is hard to sustain, however, given that the term *properties of interest* has no precise definition. (Of course, the same is true of the term *property* itself, for that matter.)

proposition A predicate with no parameters (i.e., no free variables); in other words, something that evaluates unequivocally to either TRUE or FALSE. Given an arbitrary predicate, substituting arguments for the parameters of that predicate yields a proposition.

Examples: 1. The sun is a star. 2. Neptune is a star. 3. Supplier S1 is under contract, is named Smith, has status 20, and is located in Paris. 4. There exists a city *c* such that there exists a supplier number *s#* such that the supplier with supplier number *s#* is located in city *c*. Notice that there are two variables, *s#* and *c*, in this last example; however, the variables in question are bound, not free, and the example overall still evaluates unequivocally to either TRUE or FALSE (it's either the case or not the case that at least one supplier is located in at least one city).

propositional calculus A sound, complete, and decidable formal system having to do with propositions and connectives and the inferences that can be made using such propositions and connectives. *Contrast* **predicate calculus**.

propositional logic Propositional calculus.

pseudovariable reference The use of an operational expression instead of a simple variable reference to denote a target for some update operation. *Note:* It's convenient for definitional purposes to regard pseudovariable references as if they were regular variable references (and we do so in this dictionary); in other words, pseudovariables are variables, loosely speaking.

Examples: Let CS be a variable of type CHAR with a current value of the string 'Middle', and consider the following assignment:

```
SUBSTR ( CS, 2, 1 ) = 'u' ;
```

SUBSTR here is the substring operator, and the effect of the assignment is to "zap" the second character position within CS, replacing the 'i' by a 'u' (after the update, therefore, the current value of CS is the string 'Muddle'). The expression on the left side of the assignment is a pseudovariable reference.

For a second example, let LSV be a view, defined as the restriction of relvar S to just suppliers in London, and consider the following DELETE statement:

```
DELETE LSV WHERE STATUS > 15 ;
```

Logically speaking, this DELETE is equivalent to the following:

```
DELETE ( S WHERE CITY = 'London' ) WHERE STATUS > 15 ;
```

In this expanded form, the target of the DELETE is specified as an operational expression (i.e., a pseudovariable reference). As the example suggests, therefore, updating a view is logically equivalent to updating a certain pseudovariable (thus, views are pseudovariables, loosely speaking).

QBE A relational language based on domain calculus. The name is an abbreviation for Query-By-Example.

quantifier *See* existential quantifier; universal quantifier. (Others are possible—for example, there exists exactly one of; for all but one of; there exists an odd number of; and so on—but EXISTS and FORALL are easily the ones encountered most frequently in practice.)

QUEL A relational language based on tuple calculus that at one time was a serious competitor to SQL.

query A retrieval request (i.e., a relational expression). Sometimes used, loosely, to refer to update requests also.

query rewrite *See* expression transformation.

quota query A query that imposes a desired limit, or quota, on the cardinality of the result (though the actual result might have cardinality either less than or greater than the specified quota).

Example: Here's a possible formulation of the quota query "Get the three heaviest parts" (the quota here is three):

```
WITH ( P RENAME ( WEIGHT AS WT ) ) AS t1 ,
     ( EXTEND P ADD ( COUNT ( t1 WHERE WT > WEIGHT )
                      AS #_HEAVIER ) AS t2 ,
     ( t2 WHERE #_HEAVIER < 3 ) AS t3 :
t3 { P#, PNAME, WEIGHT, COLOR, CITY }
```

Using the RANK shorthand (q.v.), we can express this query a little more succinctly as:

```
( ( RANK P BY ( DESC WEIGHT AS W ) ) WHERE W≤3 )
                      { P#, PNAME, WEIGHT, COLOR, CITY }
```

range 1. *See* function. 2. *See* range variable.

range variable Relational calculus analog of a logic variable; in other words, a variable that "ranges over" some specified set of values (either the set of tuples in some relation or the set of values of some type) and can appear either bound or free in relational calculus expressions.

RANK *See* ranking.

ranking Let r be a relation with no attribute called X. Then the ranking RANK r BY (*item*,...,*item* AS X), where each "item" consists of either ASC (ascending) or DESC (descending) followed by the name of an attribute of r (and the overall sequence of items in the commalist specifies major-to-minor ordering in the usual way), is a relation identical to r except that (a) it has an additional attribute X, and (b) the X value in any given tuple of that result shows that tuple's ranking position with respect to the specified ordering.

Example: See quota query.

read-only operator A function; i.e., an operator that, when invoked, updates nothing (except possibly variables local to the implementation of the operator in question) but returns a value, of a type declared when the operator in question is defined. A read-only operator invocation thus denotes a value; i.e., it's an expression, and it can appear wherever a literal of the appropriate type is allowed. In particular, it can be nested inside other expressions.

real relvar A base relvar or a snapshot (*contrast* virtual relvar).

recursive query A relational expression—which by definition can be thought of as the invocation of some relation-valued function *f*—whose evaluation involves further invocations of that same function *f*.

Example: Here's a recursive definition of an operator to compute the transitive closure, q.v., of a binary relation with attributes A and B, both of type P# (the code isn't very efficient, but it can obviously be improved in a variety of ways):

```
OPERATOR TRANCLO ( AB RELATION { A P#, B P# } )
              RETURNS RELATION { A P#, B P# } ;
    RETURN
  ( WITH ( AB UNION
           ( ( ( AB JOIN
                 ( ( AB RENAME ( B AS C ) )
                     RENAME ( A AS B ) ) ) { A, C })
                 RENAME ( C AS B ) ) ) AS ttt :
           IF ttt = AB THEN ttt ELSE TRANCLO ( ttt )
           END IF ) ;
  END OPERATOR ;
```

Now the invocation TRANCLO(*r*), where *r* is a relation of the appropriate type, can be thought of as a recursive query, because it implicitly involves further invocations of TRANCLO itself.

redundancy A given database displays redundancy if and only if it includes two or more distinct representations, either direct or indirect, of the same proposition. *See also* **controlled redundancy**.

referenced relvar *See* foreign key.

referencing The relational meaning of this term is described under **foreign key**; it should not be confused with the operator of the same name (found in systems that support pointers but not in relational systems) that, given a variable *V*, returns a pointer to *V*. *Note:* Systems that support pointers typically support an operator called *dereferencing* as well, which, given a pointer *p*, returns the variable that *p* points to.

referencing relvar *See* foreign key.

referential action The action specification portion of a foreign key rule (e.g., "cascade," in a DELETE rule).

referential constraint *See* foreign key.

---

referential integrity Loosely, the rule that no database is allowed to contain any unmatched foreign key values. More precisely, let *FK* be some foreign key in some referencing relvar *R2*; let *K* be the corresponding key in the corresponding referenced relvar *R1*; and let *K'* be obtained from *K* as explained in the entry for **foreign key**. Then referential integrity requires that there never be a time at which an *FK* value exists in *R2* that doesn't simultaneously exist as the *K'* value for some (necessarily unique) tuple in *R1*.

reflexive 1. *(Of a truth-valued operator)* Let *Op* be a dyadic truth-valued operator, and assume for definiteness that *Op* is expressed in infix style. Then *Op* is reflexive if and only if, for all *x*, *x Op x* is true. 2. *(Of a relation)* Let *r* be a binary relation. Then *r* is reflexive if and only if, for all *x*, the tuple <*x,x*> appears in *r*. 3. *(Of FDs) See* Armstrong's inference rules.

Examples (first definition only): The logical operator EQUIV; the "less than or equals" operator "≤".

refresh *See* snapshot.

relation A relation value. *Note:* As is well known, the term is also commonly used to refer to a relation variable, but this usage is deprecated as the source of much confusion.

relation assignment Relational assignment.

relation comparison Relational comparison.

relation constant A named relation.

Examples: TABLE_DEE and TABLE_DUM. *Note:* These two relation constants are probably built-in (i.e., system-defined)—assuming they're supported at all, that is, which in today's products they probably aren't. Here, by contrast, is one that's user-defined:

```
CONST STATES
RELATION { TUPLE { STATE NAME('Alabama') } ,
           TUPLE { STATE NAME('Alaska' ) } ,
           ..............
           TUPLE { STATE NAME('Wyoming') } } ;
```

relation equality Equality of relations; relations *r1* and *r2* are equal (i.e., the relational comparison *r1* = *r2* evaluates to TRUE) if and only if *r1* and *r2* are the very same relation.

relation expression   Relational expression.

relation predicate   Let *r* be a relation. Then the relation predicate for *r* is the predicate that represents the user-understood meaning of *r* in some particular context. If *r* is of degree *n*, that predicate will be *n*-adic (it will have a parameter for each attribute of *r*). In accordance with The Closed World Assumption, moreover, the body of *r* will contain all and only those tuples that correspond to invocations of that predicate that evaluate to TRUE.

Examples: 1. Let *r* be the projection of the current value of relvar S over S# and CITY. Then the predicate for *r* is "There exists a name *n* and a status *st* such that supplier S# is under contract, is named *n*, has status *st*, and is located in CITY." Note that this predicate is dyadic, as is to be expected for a binary relation. 2. Consider the relations *r1* and *r2*, where *r1* is the projection S{CITY} and *r2* is the projection P{CITY}. Then it's certainly possible for *r1* and *r2* to be equal; nevertheless, they have different predicates, corresponding to their two different contexts (loosely speaking, the predicates are "There exists a supplier located in CITY" and "There exists a part stored in CITY," respectively).

relation type   Let {*H*} be a heading; then RELATION {*H*} is a relation type with the same degree and attributes as {*H*}.

Examples: The type of relvar S is

```
RELATION { S# S#, SNAME NAME,
                STATUS INTEGER, CITY CHAR }
```

The following (corresponding to a certain projection of relvar S) is also a relation type:

```
RELATION { CITY CHAR, SNAME NAME }
```

relation type generator   *See* type generator.

relation type inference   The process of determining the type of the value denoted by a given relational expression. Note that this process is completely specified by the rules defining the types of the results of the various relational operations, q.v.

relation value   Loosely, a table (value). More precisely, let RELATION {*H*} be a relation type, and let {*b*} be a set of tuples of type TUPLE {H}. Let *r* be the pair <{H},{b}>. Then *r* is a relation value (relation for short) of type RELATION {H}, with heading {H} and body {b}, and the same degree and attributes as {H} and the same cardinality as {b}. *Contrast* **relation variable; relvar.** *Note:* Relations as defined in the relational model differ in certain respects from the mathematical construct of the same name. In particular, relations in mathematics typically don't have named attributes; instead, their attributes are identified by their ordinal position, left to right.

relation-valued attribute   An attribute whose type is some relation type. Values of such an attribute are relations of the specified type (sometimes called nested relations, since they're "nested" inside tuples—especially tuples in some other relation). *Note:* If a relvar has a relation-valued attribute, that fact in and of itself doesn't constitute a violation of any particular level of normalization (not even first); however, such attributes are usually contraindicated in database design, at least in base relvars, because they necessarily imply some structural asymmetry and thereby give rise to asymmetry (and complexity) in queries and updates also. *See also* **grouping; ungrouping.**

relation variable   Loosely, a table (variable); more precisely, a variable whose type is some relation type. Let relation variable *R* be of type RELATION {H}; then *R* has the same heading (and therefore attributes) and degree as that type does. Let the value of *R* at some given time be *r*; then *R* has the same body and cardinality at that time as *r* does. Note that a relation variable is *not* the same thing as a set of tuple variables (not even a set of tuple variables all of the same type). *Contrast* **relation; relation value.**

relational algebra   An open-ended collection of read-only operators on relations, each of which takes one or more relations as operands and produces a relation as a result. Exactly which operators are included is somewhat arbitrary, but the collection is required to be at least as powerful as relational calculus, in the sense that every relational calculus expression is semantically equivalent to some relational algebra expression. Also, the operators are generic, in the sense that they apply to all possible relations (loosely speaking). *Note:* Relational assignment is a relational operator too, but it isn't a relational algebra operator because it isn't read-only.

relational assignment An operation that assigns a relation value to a relation variable (of the same type).

relational calculus An applied form of predicate calculus, tailored to operating on relations, with the property that every relational calculus expression is semantically equivalent to some relational algebra expression. *See also* **domain calculus; tuple calculus.**

relational comparison A boolean expression of the form *(exp1) theta (exp2)*, where *exp1* and *exp2* are relational expressions of the same type *T* and *theta* is any comparison operator that makes sense for relations of type *T* (e.g., "=", "≠", "⊆", etc.). *Note:* The parentheses surrounding *exp1* and *exp2* in the comparison might not be needed in practice.

relational completeness A measure of the expressive power of a language. Essentially, a language is relationally complete if and only if it's at least as powerful as relational calculus—meaning that any relation that is definable by some relational calculus expression is also definable by some expression of the language in question.

Examples: Relational algebra is relationally complete, because every relational calculus expression is semantically equivalent to some relational algebra expression. It follows that in order to prove that a given language *L* is relationally complete, it suffices to prove that every relational algebra expression is semantically equivalent to some expression in *L* (which is often easier than proving that every relational calculus expression is semantically equivalent to some expression in *L*). SQL, for example, can easily be shown to be relationally complete in this way. *Note:* In fact, SQL is "more than" relationally complete, in that its expressions permit the definition of many objects that aren't relations at all.

relational database A database that abides by *The Information Principle*. We assume throughout this dictionary that databases are always relational, barring explicit statements to the contrary.

relational DBMS A DBMS that manages relational databases (and no others); equivalently, a DBMS that implements the relational model.

relational expression An expression denoting a relation. Relation literals, relation selector invocations, relcon and relvar references (i.e., relcon and relvar names, syntactically speaking), and relational algebra operator invocations are all special cases.

relational model The formal theory or foundation on which relational databases in particular and relational technology in general are based. The relational model is often loosely characterized as having three aspects: a structural aspect, which has to do with relations as such; an integrity aspect, which has to do with candidate and foreign keys; and a manipulative aspect, which has to do with operators such as join. More precisely, the relational model consists of the following components: (a) an open-ended collection of scalar types, including in particular type BOOLEAN; (b) a relation type generator and an intended interpretation for relations of types generated thereby; (c) facilities for defining relation variables of such generated relation types; (d) a relational assignment operator; and (e) an open-ended collection of generic read-only operators (i.e., relational algebra or relational calculus) for deriving relations from relations. Notice part (e) in particular; it's a far too common error to regard the relational model as consisting of structure only and to overlook the operators, and yet (as Codd once said) structure without operators is rather like anatomy without physiology. Note, moreover, that those operators aren't just meant for writing queries, as many seem to think; rather, they're for writing expressions, expressions that serve many purposes (including query but not limited to it alone). One particularly important purpose is the formulation of constraints (though in this case, the relational expression will be just a subexpression of some boolean expression, frequently though not invariably an invocation of IS_EMPTY, q.v.). *Note:* In the interest of physical data independence, the relational model is deliberately silent on everything to do with performance.

relational operator An operator that (a) takes either relations or relvars (or both) as operands and (b) either returns a relation or updates at least one relvar.

relationship 1. A term used briefly in Codd's early papers (later discarded) to mean what we would now call either a relation or a relvar, as the context demands. 2. In E/R modeling, "an association among entities" (definition taken from the original E/R paper). 3. More generally, given two sets (not necessarily distinct), a rule pairing elements of the first set with elements of the second set; equivalently, that pairing itself. This definition can easily be extended to three, four, ..., or any number of given sets; i.e., relationships aren't necessarily binary (consider, for example, the ternary relationship involving suppliers, parts, and projects mentioned in the example under **fifth normal form**).

relcon A relation constant.

relvar A relation variable. *Note:* For simplicity, we assume in this dictionary that all relvars are part of some database. However, there's no good reason why application-local relvars shouldn't be supported as well.

relvar constraint 1. *("A" relvar constraint)* An integrity constraint that refers to the relvar in question, as well as possibly others; informally, a single-relvar constraint. 2. *("The" relvar constraint)* The logical AND of all integrity constraints, apart from type constraints, that apply to a given relvar (*the* relvar constraint—sometimes called the *total* relvar constraint—for the relvar in question); in other words, the formal, system-understood "meaning" for the relvar in question. *Note:* All relvar constraints, in either sense, are also database constraints (q.v.).

Examples: First, the key constraint specified in the definition of relvar S is a relvar constraint on that relvar. Second, the foreign key constraint from SP to S is a relvar constraint on both relvar S and relvar SP. Third, here are some more relvar constraints that might apply to relvar S:

```
CONSTRAINT C1 IS_EMPTY
   ( S WHERE STATUS < 1 OR STATUS > 100 ) ;
/* status values must be in the */
/* range 1 to 100 inclusive     */

CONSTRAINT C3 IS_EMPTY
   ( ( S JOIN SP )
     WHERE STATUS < 20 AND P# = P#('P6') ) ;
/* no supplier with status less */
/* than 20 can supply part P6   */
```

(Constraint C3 is also a relvar constraint for relvar SP.)

Finally, suppose for the sake of the example that the foregoing constraints (the key constraint on relvar S, the foreign key con-

straint from relvar SP to relvar S, and constraints C1 and C3)
are the only ones that apply to relvar S. Then the logical AND
of all of them is "the" (total) relvar constraint for that relvar.

relvar predicate Let *R* be a relvar (real or virtual). Then the relvar
predicate for *R* is the predicate that represents the user-understood meaning of *R*. If *R* is of degree *n*, that predicate will be
n-adic (it will have a parameter for each attribute of *R*). In
accordance with The Closed World Assumption, moreover, at
any given time the body of *R* will contain all and only those
tuples that correspond to invocations of that predicate that
evaluate to TRUE at that time. *Contrast* **relvar constraint** (second
definition); this latter is a formal construct, but relvar predicates are necessarily somewhat informal. *Note:* Relvar predicates are sometimes called *business rules* (though some writers
use this term to include other constructs in addition to relvar
predicates).

Example: The relvar predicate for relvar S is "Supplier S# is
under contract, is named SNAME, has status STATUS, and is
located in CITY."

renaming Let *r* be a relation, let *A* be an attribute of *r*, and let *r*
not have an attribute named *B*. Then the renaming *r* RENAME
(*A* AS *B*) is a relation with (a) heading identical to that of *r*
except that attribute *A* in that heading is renamed *B*, and (b)
body identical to that of *r* except that all references to *A* in that
body are replaced by references to *B*. *See also* **tuple renaming**.

Example: The expression

```
P RENAME ( WEIGHT AS WT )
```

yields a relation identical to the current value of relvar P, except
that attribute WEIGHT is renamed WT. Note that relvar P per
se remains unaltered in the database—RENAME is not like
ALTER TABLE in SQL, it's simply a read-only operator that
(like restrict, for example) takes a certain relation as input and
returns another as output. *Note:* For reasons of user friendliness, **Tutorial D** allows two or more consecutive renamings to
be expressed by means of a single RENAME invocation. Thus,
for example, the expression (P RENAME (WEIGHT AS WT))
RENAME (COLOR AS COL) can be abbreviated to P
RENAME (WEIGHT AS WT, COLOR AS COL). A similar

remark applies to several other relational (and tuple) operations also—for example, EXTEND, SUMMARIZE, and so on.

repeating group Let some table have a column *C* of type *T*. Then *C* is a repeating group column if and only if the values appearing within *C* aren't values of type *T* but are, rather, sets (or lists or arrays or ...) of values of type *T*. Repeating groups are outlawed in the relational model (which is why this definition is phrased in terms of tables and columns instead of relations and attributes); in fact, a "relation" with a repeating group "attribute" is a contradiction in terms.

restriction Let *bx* be a boolean expression in which all of the attributes mentioned are attributes of the same relation *r*. Then the restriction *r* WHERE *bx* is a relation with heading the same as that of *r* and body consisting of all tuples of *r* for which *bx* evaluates to TRUE. *Note:* Restriction is sometimes known as selection, but it shouldn't be confused with the SELECT operation of SQL. The SQL SELECT operation—meaning, more specifically, just the SELECT portion of an SQL SELECT - FROM - WHERE expression—can be loosely characterized as a combination of EXTEND, RENAME, and "project" ("project" in quotes because it doesn't eliminate duplicates, in general, unless explicitly requested to do so via DISTINCT).

Example: The following expression denotes a restriction of the relation that's the current value of relvar P:

```
P WHERE WEIGHT < WEIGHT ( 17.5 ) AND CITY = 'Paris'
```

reversible decomposition Replacing a relvar *R* by a set of relvars *R1, R2, ..., Rn* in such a way that it's guaranteed that *R* can be obtained from *R1, R2, ..., Rn*. Nonloss decomposition, q.v., is an important special case.

RM/T An extended form of the relational model, due to Codd, with the explicit goal of capturing more meaning than the relational model per se is capable of. The name is an abbreviation for Relational Model / Tasmania (so called because Codd first described it at a conference in Tasmania). RM/T includes a variety of "semantic" constructs (e.g., E- and P-relations, which are meant to represent entities and properties, respectively, together with operators for operating on such relations). RM/T has never been implemented in a commercial product (in fact it couldn't be, since the sole formal paper on the topic— "Extending the Database Relational Model to Capture More Meaning," *ACM TODS 4*, No. 4—fails to specify it adequately), but its ideas can be useful as an aid in conventional database design.

RM/V1 *See* RM/V2.

RM/V2 Codd spent much of the late 1980s revising and extending the original relational model, which he referred to as "the relational model Version 1" or RM/V1, to produce "the relational model Version 2" or RM/V2. As noted in the introduction, however, definitions in this dictionary are intended to conform to the relational model as defined by *The Third Manifesto*; as a consequence, they don't always agree with Codd's RM/V1 or RM/V2 definitions. For details of these latter, see Codd's book *The Relational Model for Database Management Version 2* (Addison-Wesley).

row 1. SQL analog of either a tuple value or a tuple variable, as the context demands. 2. More generally, a picture of a tuple (on paper, for example). *See also* **table**.

row ID An implementation construct (typically, though not necessarily, some kind of pointer, q.v.). In some commercial products, however, such IDs are exposed to the user—usually, and unfortunately, in such a way as to violate either *The Information Principle* or *The Principle of Interchangeability* or both. Sometimes called a tuple ID.

RVA Relation-valued attribute.

scalar 1. *(Of a type, attribute, value, or variable)* Having no user-visible component parts. The term is also often used as an abbreviation for *scalar value* specifically. 2. *(Of an operator)* Returning a scalar result. *Note:* Scalar types and scalar values are required in the relational model; scalar variables aren't, but they're almost certainly needed in the external environment in order to support, for example, retrieval of the value of some scalar attribute from some tuple of some relation. Note too that there's no such thing as "absolute scalarness"—the concept is necessarily somewhat relative. For example, a phone number might be perceived equally well as an indivisible scalar value or as a tuple value consisting of country code, area code, and local number (and a database design involving phone numbers ought to support both perceptions). Consider also the case of TABLE_DUM, which is clearly a relation and yet (like a scalar) has no user-visible component parts.

second normal form Relvar *R* is in second normal form, 2NF, if and only if every attribute *A* of *R* not contained in any key of *R* is such that the set {*A*} is irreducibly dependent on every key of *R*. Every 2NF relvar is in 1NF (as is every relvar, in fact). *Note:* Although being in 2NF clearly doesn't preclude being in the next higher normal form (3NF) as well, the term *2NF* is often used loosely to refer to a relvar that's in 2NF and not in 3NF. Also, second normal form as such is no longer very important (BCNF, 5NF, and 6NF being the normal forms of most practical significance); we mention it here mainly for historical reasons.

Example: As noted under **Boyce/Codd normal form**, it's often more instructive with the normal forms to show a counterexample rather than an example per se. Suppose for the sake of the example, therefore, that relvar SP has an additional attribute CITY, representing the city of the applicable supplier. This revised version of SP satisfies the FD {S#} → {CITY}, and is therefore not in 2NF (because CITY isn't contained in any key and {CITY} isn't irreducibly dependent on the key {S#,P#}).

second order logic A form of predicate logic in which the sets over which variables range are allowed to contain predicates. *Contrast* **first order logic**.

Example: Consider the well-known principle of mathematical induction, limited here for simplicity to its application to monadic predicates *p* whose sole parameter is of type "nonnegative integer." That principle can be stated (in somewhat stilted English) as follows: for all such predicates *p*, if (a) $p(0)$ is true and if (b) for all *i*, if $p(i)$ is true then $p(i+1)$ is true, then (c) $p(n)$ is true for all *n*. In symbols:

```
FORALL p ( ( p(0) AND
                 FORALL i ( p(i) IMPLIES p(i+1) ) )
         IMPLIES FORALL n ( p(n) ) )
```

In this example, the variables *i* and *n* range over nonnegative integers but the variable *p* ranges over predicates (specifically, monadic predicates whose sole parameter is of type "nonnegative integer"). The overall expression is thus second order.

selection *See* restriction.

selector An operator for selecting, or specifying, an arbitrary value of a given type; not to be confused with the SELECT operation of SQL (for a loose characterization of this latter, *see* restriction). Every type, tuple and relation types included, has at least one associated selector. *Note:* Ultimately, the only way any expression can ever yield a value of type *T* is via invocation of some selector for that type *T*. In fact, the selector notion is essentially a generalization of the familiar concept of a literal; that is, all literals are selector invocations, but some selector invocations aren't literals. (To be specific, a selector invocation is a literal if and only if all of its arguments are literals in turn.)

Examples: Several selector invocations appear in the example under INSERT; however, those examples are all literals, since their arguments are all literals in turn. By contrast, here are some selector invocations that aren't literals. Let SX, PX, and QX be variables of types CHAR, CHAR, and INTEGER, respectively. Then (a) the expressions S#(SX), P#(PX), and QTY(QX) are selector invocations for types S#, P#, and QTY, respectively; (b) the expression TUPLE {S# S#(SX), P# P#(PX), QTY QTY(150)} is a selector invocation for tuple type TUPLE {S# S#, P# P#, QTY QTY}; and (c) the expression RELATION {*ts*}, where *ts* is the tuple selector invocation just shown, is a selector invocation for relation type RELATION {S# S#, P# P#, QTY QTY}.

self-referencing relvar A relvar *R* with a foreign key matching some key of *R* itself. Database designs involving such relvars are usually contraindicated.

semantic optimization Using integrity constraints to help in the process of transforming relational expressions, usually for performance purposes. *See* expression transformation; optimizer.

Examples: Consider the query

```
P WHERE CITY = 'London' AND COLOR = 'Red'
```

Suppose relvar P is subject to the constraint that parts in London must be red. Then the query can clearly be transformed into the following simpler one:

```
P WHERE CITY = 'London'
```

Moreover, if the original query had requested blue parts instead of red ones, the optimizer might be able to determine that the result must be empty without actually having to execute the query at all.

semidifference Let *r1* and *r2* be relations. Then the semidifference between *r1* and *r2* (in that order), *r1* NOT MATCHING *r2*, is shorthand for *r1* MINUS (*r1* MATCHING *r2*).

Example: The expression

```
S NOT MATCHING SP
```

yields suppliers who currently supply no parts at all.

SEMIJOIN Same as MATCHING.

semijoin Let *r1* and *r2* be relations. Then the semijoin of *r1* with *r2* (in that order), *r1* MATCHING *r2*, is shorthand for (*r1* JOIN *r2*){*X*}, where {*X*} is the heading of *r1*. Note that, in general, *r1* MATCHING *r2* and r2 MATCHING *r1* aren't equivalent.

Example: The expression

```
S MATCHING SP
```

yields suppliers who currently supply at least one part.

SEMIMINUS Same as NOT MATCHING.

sentence *See* logical system.

SEQUEL Original name for SQL.

set A collection of objects, called elements, with the property that given an arbitrary object *x*, one can determine whether *x* appears in the collection (*see* set membership). Sets have no ordering to their elements, nor do they contain any duplicate elements. *Note:* There's a logical difference (actually a difference in type) between an element *x* and the set {*x*} that contains only that element *x*. Thus, a relational language needs to provide both (a) an operator for extracting the single tuple from a relation of cardinality one, and (b) an operator for extracting the single attribute value from a tuple of degree one (*see* **attribute extractor**; **tuple extractor**). Note too that the inverse functionality—in effect, building up a tuple from specified attribute values and building up a relation from specified tuple values—is provided by the appropriate tuple and relation selectors (*see* **selector**).

set function Deprecated (because inappropriate) term for an aggregate operator.

set inclusion Set *s2* is included in set *s1* if and only if it is a subset of *s1*. Note that every set is included in itself, also that every set includes the empty set.

set level The operators of the relational model are all set level, in the sense that they take entire relations or relvars (or both) as operands and either produce entire relations as results or update entire relvars. (*Relation level* would be a better term.) *Contrast* **tuple level**.

set membership (*Of an element*) The property of appearing in some given set; the operation of testing for that property. Set membership is usually denoted by the symbol "$\in$"; thus, for example, the boolean expression $x \in s$ (which is semantically equivalent to the expression $\{x\} \subseteq s$) returns TRUE if and only if element x does in fact appear in set s.

set theory A branch of mathematics, closely related to logic, that deals with the nature of sets; it formalizes the concept of a set in terms of certain axioms, such as the axiom of extension ("Sets *s1* and *s2* are equal if and only if they have the same elements").

Sheffer stroke *See* **NAND**.

simple attribute An attribute. *Contrast* **composite attribute**.

simple predicate A predicate that involves no connectives.

simple proposition A proposition that involves no connectives.

single-relvar constraint Informally, an integrity constraint that mentions exactly one relvar. *Contrast* **multi-relvar constraint**. *Note:* The difference between single- and multi-relvar constraints is more a matter of pragma than logic, thanks to *The Principle of Interchangeability*.

Examples: The key constraints for relvars S, SP, and P; also constraints C1 and C2 from the examples under **database constraint**.

sixth normal form Relvar *R* is in sixth normal form, 6NF, if and only if it can't be nonloss decomposed at all (other than into the identity projection of *R*). Observe, therefore, that 6NF is the ultimate normal form with respect to normalization as conventionally understood; in particular, every 6NF relvar is in 5NF. *Note:* The concept of 6NF is given an extended definition in a temporal database context, where it enjoys certain advantages over 5NF—advantages that don't necessarily apply in a conventional (nontemporal) database. The details are beyond the scope of this dictionary.

Example: Relvars S and P aren't in 6NF, because they can both be nonloss decomposed into several binary projections. By contrast, relvar SP is in 6NF.

snapshot A derived relvar that's real, not virtual (*contrast* **view**). The value of a given snapshot at a given time is the result of evaluating a certain relational expression (the snapshot-defining expression, specified when the snapshot per se is defined) at some time prior to the time in question. The snapshot is "refreshed" (meaning the snapshot-defining expression is reevaluated and the result assigned as the new current value of the snapshot) on demand or, more usually, when some specific event occurs, such as the passing of a certain interval of time. *Note:* The snapshot-defining expression must mention at least one relvar, for otherwise the snapshot wouldn't be, specifically, a relation variable.

Example: The following statement defines a snapshot called LSS:

```
VAR LSS SNAPSHOT ( S WHERE CITY = 'London' )
        REFRESH EVERY DAY ;
```

The relation that's the current value of snapshot LSS at any given time is equal to the value of the snapshot-defining expression S WHERE CITY = 'London' as it was at most 24 hours prior to the time in question.

sort/merge A join implementation technique.

soundness The property of a formal system according to which, given a set *s* of sentences of the system, no sentence not implied by those in *s* can be derived using the rules of inference of that system (i.e., all theorems are tautologies). *Contrast* **completeness**.

SQL The best-known attempt (unfortunately a seriously flawed one) to realize the abstract ideas of the relational model in concrete syntactic form. The name SQL—the official pronunciation is "ess cue ell," though it's often pronounced "sequel"— was originally an abbreviation for *Structured Query Language*. In its standard incarnation, however, the name is just a name and isn't considered to be an abbreviation for anything at all. The version of the SQL standard current at the time of this writing is SQL:2003 (so called because it was ratified in 2003); the next version is scheduled for ratification in 2007.

star join A join implementation technique.

state constraint A database constraint that is not a transition constraint.

statement 1. *(Logic)* A proposition. 2. *(Programming languages)* A construct that causes some action to occur, such as defining or updating a variable or changing the flow of control. *Contrast* **expression**.

subexpression An expression nested inside another expression.

subquery Loosely, a subexpression of a relational expression; in SQL, a SELECT - FROM - WHERE expression nested inside another such.

subject to update Let *Op* be an update operator that, when invoked, updates the argument corresponding to parameter *x*. Then parameter *x* is said to be subject to update (and any argument corresponding to *x* must be a variable specifically).

Example: See the second version of operator DOUBLE in the examples under **argument**.

subset Set *s2* is a subset of set *s1* if and only if every element of *s2* is also an element of *s1*. Observe that every set is a subset of itself, also that the empty set is a subset of every set. *Contrast* **proper subset**.

substitution 1. *(View implementation)* A technique for implementing operations on views, according to which references to view *V* are replaced by the view-defining expression for *V* (*contrast* **materialization**). 2. *(Operator invocation)* The process of replacing a parameter by an argument.

Example (view implementation): See the second example under pseudovariable reference.

subtables and supertables A scheme according to which some table *T1* is specified to have all of the columns of some other table *T2,* together with certain additional columns of its own (*see* table). One of the numerous reasons for deprecating any such scheme is that which of T1 and T2 is regarded as the subtable and which the supertable can depend on the system in question.

subtuple A subset of a tuple; hence, a tuple.

subtype *See* type inheritance.

summarization Let *r1* and *r2* be relations such that *r2* is of the same type as some projection of *r1,* and let the attributes of *r2* be *A1, A2, ..., An.* Then the summarization SUMMARIZE *r1* PER (*r2*) ADD (*summary* AS *X*) is a relation with (a) heading the heading of *r2* extended with attribute *X,* and (b) body consisting of all tuples *t* such that *t* is a tuple of *r2* extended with a value *x* for attribute *X.* That value *x* is computed by evaluating *summary* over all tuples of *r1* that have the same value for attributes *A1, A2, ..., An* as tuple *t* does. Relation *r2* must not have an attribute called *X,* and *summary* must not refer to *X.* *Note:* If *r2* is not just of the same type as some projection of *r1* but actually is such a projection, the PER clause can be replaced by a BY clause, as shown in the third of the following examples.

Example: The following expression denotes a summarization of the relation that's the current value of relvar SP:

```
SUMMARIZE SP PER ( S { S# } ) ADD ( COUNT ( ) AS CT )
```

That summarization is a relation of type RELATION {S# S#, CT INTEGER}, containing one tuple for each distinct S# value currently appearing in relvar S (not SP!—note the PER specification), and no other tuples. Given the sample values in Figure 1, for example, the tuple for supplier S2 in the result has S# value S2 and CT value two, and the tuple for supplier S5 has S# value S5 and CT value zero. By contrast, the expression

```
SUMMARIZE SP PER ( SP { S# } ) ADD ( COUNT ( ) AS CT )
```

yields a relation of type RELATION {S# S#, CT INTEGER} with one tuple for each distinct S# value currently appearing in relvar SP. Given the sample values in Figure 1, for example, the result contains no tuple for supplier S5. *Note:* This second SUMMARIZE example can be simplified slightly thus:

```
SUMMARIZE SP BY { S# } ADD ( COUNT ( ) AS CT )
```

SUMMARIZE *See* summarization.

summary A SUMMARIZE operand (*see* **summarization**). Note carefully that summaries aren't aggregate operator invocations, though they might look rather like them. An aggregate operator invocation is an expression, and it can appear wherever a literal of the appropriate type can appear. A summary, by contrast, is merely an operand to SUMMARIZE; it isn't an expression, it has no meaning outside the context of SUMMARIZE, and in fact can't appear outside that context.

superkey Loosely, a superset of a key; it has the uniqueness property but not necessarily the irreducibility property. More precisely, let *K* be a subset of the heading of relvar *R*; then *K* is a superkey for *R* if and only if no possible value for *R* contains two distinct tuples with the same value for *K*.

Examples: For relvar S, {S#} and {S#,CITY} are both superkeys. Note that the heading of any given relvar *R* is necessarily a superkey for *R*.

superset Set *s1* is a superset of set *s2* if and only if every element of *s2* is also an element of *s1*. Note that every set is a superset of itself, also that every set is a superset of the empty set. *Contrast* **proper superset.**

supertype *See* type inheritance.

surjection A mapping, or function, from set *s1* to set *s2* such that each element of *s2* is the image of at least one element of *s1* (in other words, a many-to-one correspondence, in the strict sense of that term). Also known as a surjective or "many-to-one onto" mapping.

Example: Let *s1* and *s2* be the set of all integers and the set of all nonnegative integers, respectively. Then the mapping from integers *x* to their absolute values |*x*| is a surjection from *s1* to *s2*.

surrogate key A single-attribute key with the property that its values serve solely as surrogates—hence the name—for the entities they stand for (in other words, they serve merely to represent the fact that the corresponding entities exist, and they carry absolutely no additional information or meaning). *Contrast* intelligent key.

symmetric 1. *(Of a truth-valued operator)* Let *Op* be a dyadic truth-valued operator, and assume for definiteness that *Op* is expressed in infix style. Then *Op* is symmetric if and only if, for all *x* and *y*, if *x Op y* is true, then so is *y Op x* (i.e., *Op* is symmetric if and only if it's commutative). 2. *(Of a relation)* Let *r* be a binary relation. Then *r* is symmetric if and only if, for all *x* and *y*, if the tuple <*x,y*> appears in *r*, then so does the tuple <*y,x*>.

Examples (first definition only): The logical operator EQUIV; the equality operator "=".

symmetric difference (set theory) The set of all elements appearing in either but not both of two given sets.

table 1. SQL analog of either a relation or a relvar, as the context demands. Here are some of the major differences between tables in SQL and their relational counterparts: (a) SQL tables can contain duplicate rows; (b) SQL tables can contain nulls; (c) SQL tables have a left-to-right column sequence; (d) SQL tables can have two or more columns with the same name; (e) SQL tables can have what are, in effect, columns with no name at all. 2. More generally, a picture of a relation (on paper, for example). *Note:* A confusion between relations and such tabular pictures probably accounts for the popular misconception that "relations are flat," or two-dimensional. While it's obviously true that those pictures are two-dimensional, relations in general aren't; rather, a relation of degree *n* is *n*-dimensional, in the sense that its tuples correspond to points in some *n*-dimensional space (one dimension for each attribute of the relation in question). One specific consequence of such considerations is that (again contrary to popular opinion) relations are perfectly capable of representing so-called multidimensional data and thereby supporting so-called online analytical processing (OLAP).

table alias *See* alias.

TABLE_DEE and TABLE_DUM Two preferably built-in relation constants. TABLE_DEE is the unique relation with no attributes and exactly one tuple (necessarily the empty tuple); TABLE_DUM is the unique relation with no attributes and no tuples at all. *Note:* The names are perhaps not very well chosen, because these two relations are precisely the ones that are most difficult to picture as tables.

tables and views / tables or views Phrases that often appear in SQL contexts and strongly suggest that views are somehow different from tables. But the whole point about views is that (in SQL terms) they *are* tables—just as, in mathematics, the whole point about a set that's (e.g.) the union or intersection of two other sets is that it is itself a set. Views should "look and feel" just like base tables to the user (*The Principle of Interchangeability* translated into SQL terms).

tautology A predicate whose every possible invocation is guaranteed to yield TRUE, regardless of what arguments are substituted for its parameters. *Contrast* **contradiction**.

Examples: Let *p1* be the predicate (actually a proposition) $2+2 = 4$; let *p2* be the predicate $x = x$, where x is an arbitrary integer; and let *p3* be the predicate (p) OR $(\text{NOT}(p))$, where p is an arbitrary predicate. Then *p1*, *p2*, and *p3* are all tautologies.

TCLOSE *See* transitive closure.

temporal database A database in which at least one of the relvars is temporal (where a temporal relvar is one whose heading includes at least one attribute of some timestamp type, implying that the corresponding relvar predicate has at least one parameter of some timestamp type). A variety of special operators can be defined to help with the management of such databases—see the book *Temporal Data and the Relational Model*, by C. J. Date, Hugh Darwen, and Nikos A. Lorentzos (Morgan Kaufmann, 2003)—but all of those operators are, in the final analysis, shorthand for something that can already be expressed in the classical relational algebra. Further details are beyond the scope of this dictionary.

theorem Something that follows from given axioms according to given rules of inference (and is therefore true if the axioms are true and the inference rules are valid). In a database, tuples in derived relations can be regarded as theorems, because they represent propositions derived from the ones represented by tuples in the base relations. Theorems include axioms (q.v.) as a degenerate special case.

theta join A relational operation, equivalent to an expression of the form (*r1* TIMES *r2*) WHERE *A1 theta A2*, where (a) *A1* and *A2* are attributes (of the same type *T*) of *r1* and *r2*, respectively, and (b) *theta* is any comparison operator that makes sense for values of type *T* (e.g., "=", ">", etc.).

Examples: The following expression represents the greater-than join (i.e., theta here is ">") of suppliers and parts over cities:

```
( ( S RENAME ( CITY AS SC ) ) TIMES
  ( P RENAME ( CITY AS PC ) ) ) WHERE SC > PC
```

We assume here that CHAR—the type of attribute CITY—is an ordinal type (">" presumably means "greater in alphabetic ordering"). Note that we could replace TIMES by JOIN in the foregoing expression without changing the meaning. Also, replacing ">" by "<" would yield a less-than join; replacing it by "=" would yield an equijoin.

third normal form Relvar *R* is in third normal form, 3NF, if and only if for every nontrivial FD *A* → *B* satisfied by *R*, either *A* is a superkey for *R* or *B* is a subset of some key of *R* (or both). Every 3NF relvar is in 2NF. *Note:* Many of the definitions of "3NF" in the literature are actually definitions of BCNF; *caveat lector.* Also, although being in 3NF clearly doesn't preclude being in the next higher normal form (BCNF) as well, the term *3NF* is often used loosely to refer to a relvar that's in 3NF and not in BCNF. In any case, third normal form as such is no longer very important (BCNF, 5NF, and 6NF being the normal forms of most practical significance); we mention it here mainly for historical reasons.

Example: As noted under **Boyce/Codd normal form**, it's often more instructive with the normal forms to show a counterexample rather than an example per se. Suppose, therefore, that relvar S satisfies the additional FD {CITY} → {STATUS}; i.e., the status for a given supplier is a function of that supplier's location. Because {CITY} isn't a superkey and {STATUS} isn't a subset of any key, this version of relvar S isn't in 3NF (though it is in 2NF).

three-valued logic A logic, abbreviated 3VL, in which there are three truth values: TRUE, FALSE, and an intermediate value usually called UNKNOWN. SQL is based on such a logic.

(The relational model, by contrast, is based on two-valued logic, q.v.) In particular, SQL's support for nulls, q.v., is based on a three-valued logic, though in fact that support is logically flawed; for example, SQL treats the UNKNOWN truth value and null as identical, even though there's a logical difference between the two—UNKNOWN is a value, while null isn't a value at all but a "mark." (This is just one of many logical errors in SQL's 3VL support.) *Note:* Tautologies in 2VL aren't necessarily tautologies in 3VL; likewise, contradictions in 2VL aren't necessarily contradictions in 3VL. As a result, theorems that hold in 2VL don't necessarily hold in 3VL, and expression transformations that are valid in 2VL aren't necessarily valid in 3VL.

time-varying relation   Codd's original term for a relvar; the term is deprecated because relations are values and therefore don't vary over time.

TIMES   *See* cartesian product.

total database constraint   *See* database constraint.

total relvar constraint   *See* relvar constraint.

transaction   A unit of recovery and concurrency; loosely, a unit of work. Transactions are all or nothing, in the sense that they either execute in their entirety or have no effect. *Note:* Transactions are often said to be a unit of integrity also. Because the relational model requires all integrity checking to be immediate, however, the unit of integrity as far as the relational model is concerned is the statement, not the transaction. *See* atomic statement; immediate checking.

transition constraint   A database constraint that limits the transitions that a given database can validly make from one state to another. *Contrast* state constraint.

Example ("No supplier's status must ever decrease"):

```
CONSTRAINT TRC1 IS_EMPTY (
( ( S' { S#, STATUS } RENAME ( STATUS AS STATUS' ) )
  JOIN
  ( S { S#, STATUS } ) )
WHERE STATUS' > STATUS ) ;
```

This formulation relies on the convention that a primed relvar name such as S' refers to the corresponding relvar as it was prior to the update under consideration.

transitive   1. *(Of a truth-valued operator)* Let *Op* be a dyadic truth-valued operator, and assume for definiteness that *Op* is expressed in infix style. Then *Op* is transitive if and only if, for all *x, y,* and *z,* if *x Op y* and *y Op z* are both true, then so is *x Op z.* 2. *(Of a relation)* Let *r* be a binary relation. Then *r* is transitive if and only if, for all *x, y,* and *z,* if the tuples $\langle x,y \rangle$ and $\langle y,z \rangle$ both appear in *r,* then so does the tuple $\langle x,z \rangle$. 3. *(Of FDs)* See Armstrong's inference rules.

Examples (first definition only): The logical operator IMPLIES; the "less than" operator "<".

transitive closure   Let *r* be a binary relation with attributes *A* and *B,* both of type *T.* Then the transitive closure of *r,* TCLOSE *r,* is a relation *r+* defined as follows: the tuple $\langle a,b \rangle$ appears in *r+* if and only if it appears in *r* or there exists a value *c* of type *T* such that the tuple $\langle a,c \rangle$ appears in *r* and the tuple $\langle c,b \rangle$ appears in *r+* (note that this is a recursive definition). As the following pseudocode algorithm suggests, computing TCLOSE *r* conceptually involves iterative formation of the union of some intermediate result (computed on the previous iteration) and a new partial result (computed on the current iteration), until that union ceases to grow—in other words, until it reaches a fixed point or "fixpoint."

```
r+ := r ;
do until r+ ceases to grow ;
   r+ := WITH ( r+ RENAME ( B AS C ) ) AS t1 ,
            ( r  RENAME ( A AS C ) ) AS t2 :
         r+ UNION ( ( t1 JOIN t2 ) { A, B } ) ;
end do;
```

transitive FD   Let relvar *R* satisfy the FDs $A \rightarrow B$ and $B \rightarrow C$; then *R* also satisfies the transitive FD $A \rightarrow C$.

TransRelational™ Model   A proprietary DBMS implementation technology, not based on conventional direct image techniques.

TRC   Tuple relational calculus.

triggered procedure   Strictly, an action (the "triggered action") to be performed if a specified event (the "triggering event") occurs, though the term is often used loosely to include the triggering event as well. No triggered procedures are prescribed by the relational model, but they aren't necessarily proscribed either (though they would be if they could lead to a violation of *The Assignment Principle*, q.v., which they very well might in practice). Foreign key rules provide a pragmatically important example (in which, as it happens, the "procedure" is specified declaratively). *Note:* The combination of a triggering event and the corresponding triggered action is often known simply as a trigger.

trivial FD   An FD that can't possibly be violated. The FD $A \to B$ is trivial if and only if A is a superset of B.

trivial JD   A JD that can't possibly be violated. The JD $*\{A1,A2,\dots, An\}$ is trivial if and only if at least one of $A1, A2,\dots, An$ is the entire heading of the pertinent relvar R.

trivial MVD   An MVD that can't possibly be violated. The MVD $A \to\to B$ is trivial if and only if either A is a superset of B or the set theory union of A and B is the heading of the pertinent relvar R (or both).

TRUE   *See* boolean value.

truth value   In two-valued logic, either TRUE or FALSE; in other words, a boolean value.

truth-valued expression   A boolean expression.

tuple   A tuple value. Every subset of a tuple (i.e., every subtuple of the tuple in question) is itself a tuple.

tuple assignment   An operation that assigns a tuple value to a tuple variable (of the same type).

tuple calculus   A version of relational calculus, semantically equivalent to domain calculus (q.v.), in which the range variables range over relations and thus denote tuples from those relations.

Example: Here's a tuple calculus formulation of the query "get supplier names for suppliers who supply at least one part" (*see* **domain calculus** for a domain calculus analog):

```
SX  RANGES OVER { S } ;
SPX RANGES OVER { SP } ;

SX.SNAME WHERE EXISTS SPX ( SPX.S# = SX.S# )
```

In stilted English: "get names of suppliers SX where there exists a shipment SPX with the same supplier number as SX."

tuple comparison A boolean expression of the form (*exp1*) *theta* (*exp2*), where *exp1* and *exp2* are tuple expressions of the same type and *theta* is either "=" or "≠" (note that the operators "<" and ">" are explicitly not defined for tuples). *Note:* The parentheses enclosing *exp1* and *exp2* in the comparison might not be needed in practice.

tuple component An <attribute, attribute value> pair appearing in the tuple in question. Note that attributes in turn are defined to be <attribute name, type name> pairs.

Examples: The pairs <<S#,S#>,S1> and <<SNAME,NAME>, Smith> are both components of the supplier tuple for supplier S1 in Figure 1. *Note:* In **Tutorial D**, tuple components are specified more simply as <attribute name, attribute value> pairs (not meant to be exact **Tutorial D** syntax). This simplified form is acceptable because the relational model requires attribute names to be unique within the pertinent heading, and those names thus effectively imply the corresponding type names.

tuple difference *See* tuple union.

tuple composition The tuple composition of tuples *t1* and *t2*, *t1* COMPOSE *t2*, is the tuple union of *t1* and *t2*, projected over all attributes not common to *t1* and *t2*.

tuple equality Equality of tuples; tuples *t1* and *t2* are equal (i.e., the tuple comparison *t1* = *t2* evaluates to TRUE) if and only if *t1* and *t2* are the very same tuple. More specifically, tuples *t1* and *t2* are equal if and only if they have the same attributes *A1*, *A2*, ..., *An*—in other words, they're of the same type— and, for all *i* (*i* = 1, 2, ..., *n*), the value *v1* of *Ai* in *t1* is equal to the value *v2* of *Ai* in *t2*. *Note:* The importance of this concept can hardly be overstated, because so much in the relational model depends on it. For example, candidate keys, foreign keys, and most—if not all—of the operators of relational algebra are defined in terms of it. Note in particular too that (speaking rather loosely) all 0-tuples are equal to one another, since in fact there's only one such tuple.

tuple expression An expression denoting a tuple.

tuple extension Let *t* be a tuple. Then the tuple extension EXTEND *t* ADD (*exp* AS *X*) is a tuple identical to *t* except that it has an additional attribute called *X*, with value as specified by *exp*. Tuple *t* must not have an attribute called *X*, and *exp* must not refer to *X*.

Example: Let *t* be some tuple from relvar P. Then the expression

```
EXTEND t ADD ( WEIGHT * 454 AS GMWT )
```

yields a tuple just like *t*, except that it has an additional attribute GMWT ("gram weight") whose value is 454 times the WEIGHT value in that same tuple.

tuple extractor An operator for extracting the single tuple from a specified relation of cardinality one.

Example: The following expression extracts the supplier tuple for supplier S1 from the current value of relvar S:

```
TUPLE FROM ( S WHERE S# = S#('S1') )
```

A runtime error will occur if the TUPLE FROM argument has cardinality either zero or two or more.

TUPLE FROM **Tutorial D** syntax for a tuple extractor (q.v.).

tuple ID *See* row ID.

tuple intersection *See* tuple union.

tuple join *See* tuple union.

tuple level An operator is tuple level if it takes individual tuples or tuplevars (or both) as operands and either produces a tuple as a result or updates a tuple variable. *Note:* There are no tuple level operations in the relational model as such, but such operations are likely to be needed in the external environment in order to support, for example, extraction of some tuple from some relation.

tuple projection Let *t* be a tuple and let {*X*} be a subset of the heading of *t*. Then the tuple projection *t*{*X*} is a tuple obtained from *t* by discarding all components not corresponding to attributes in {*X*}.

Example: Let t be some tuple from relvar S. Then the expression $t\{STATUS,CITY\}$ yields a tuple of type TUPLE {STATUS INTEGER, CITY CHAR}, containing just the STATUS and CITY components from that tuple t.

tuple relational calculus Tuple calculus.

tuple renaming Let t be a tuple, let A be an attribute of t, and let t not have an attribute named B. Then the tuple renaming t RENAME (A AS B) is a tuple identical to t except that attribute A in that tuple is renamed B.

Example: Let t be some tuple from relvar P. Then the expression

```
t RENAME ( WEIGHT AS WT )
```

yields a tuple just like t, except that attribute WEIGHT is renamed WT.

tuple type Let $\{H\}$ be a heading; then TUPLE $\{H\}$ is a tuple type with the same degree and attributes as $\{H\}$.

Examples: The type of the tuples in relvar S is

```
TUPLE { S# S#, SNAME NAME, STATUS INTEGER, CITY CHAR }
```

The following (corresponding to a certain projection of a supplier tuple) is also a tuple type:

```
TUPLE { CITY CHAR, SNAME NAME }
```

tuple type generator *See* type generator.

tuple type inference The process of determining the type of the value denoted by a given tuple expression. Note that this process is completely specified by the rules defining the types of the results of the various tuple operations, q.v.

tuple union The tuple union of two tuples $t1$ and $t2$, $t1$ UNION $t2$ (where if $t1$ and $t2$ have any attributes in common, then the corresponding attribute values must be the same), is the set theory union of $t1$ and $t2$. (This operation could obviously be generalized to apply to any number of tuples.) *Note:* Tuple union might reasonably be called tuple join. Also, it would clearly be possible to define tuple intersection and tuple difference operators if desired.

Example: Let $t1$ be a tuple from relvar S and $t2$ a tuple from relvar SP, and let $t1$ and $t2$ have the same S# component (the same S# value in particular). Then the expression *t1* UNION *t2* yields a tuple of type TUPLE {S# S#, SNAME NAME, STATUS INTEGER, CITY CHAR, P# P#, QTY QTY}, with components as in *t1* or *t2* or both, as applicable.

tuple unwrapping Let *s* be a tuple with an attribute *YT* of type TUPLE {*Y*}, and let {*X*} be the set of all attributes of *s* except *YT*. Let {*Y*} have attributes *Y1*, *Y2*, ..., *Yn*; also, let {*X*} not contain any attribute with the same name as any of *Y1*, *Y2*, ..., *Yn*. Then the tuple unwrapping *s* UNWRAP (*YT*) is another tuple *t*. The heading of *t* consists of the set theory union of {*X*} and {*Y*}. Let tuple *s* have *X* value *x* and *YT* value a tuple with *Y1* value *y1*, *Y2* value *y2*, ..., and *Yn* value *yn*; then tuple *t* has *X* value *x*, *Y1* value *y1*, *Y2* value *y2*, ..., and *Yn* value *yn*.

Example: Let *t* be a tuple from relvar SP, and let *tw* be the tuple resulting from the expression

```
t WRAP ( { P#, QTY } AS PQ_TUP )
```

(*see* **tuple wrapping**). Then the expression

```
tw UNWRAP ( PQ_TUP )
```

yields *t*.

tuple value Loosely, a row (value). More precisely, let TUPLE {*H*} be a tuple type, and let *t* be a set of pairs <<*A,T*>,*v*>, called components, obtained from {*H*} by attaching to each attribute <*A,T*> in {*H*} some value *v* of type *T*, called the attribute value in *t* for attribute *A*. Then *t* is a tuple value (tuple for short) of type TUPLE {*H*}, with heading {*H*} and the same degree and attributes as {*H*}. *Note:* Tuples as defined in the relational model differ in certain respects from the mathematical construct of the same name. In particular, tuples in mathematics typically don't have named attributes; instead, their attributes are identified by their ordinal position, left to right.

tuple variable Loosely, a row (variable); more precisely, a variable whose type is some tuple type. Let tuple variable *T* be of type TUPLE {*H*}; then *T* has the same heading (and therefore attributes) and degree as that type does. *Note:* Tuple variables aren't required by the relational model as such, but they're likely to be needed in the external environment in order to support, for example, extraction of some tuple from some relation.

tuple wrapping Let *t* be a tuple and let the heading of *t* be partitioned into subsets {*X*} and {*Y*}. Let the attributes of {*Y*} be *Y1, Y2, …, Yn*; also, let {*X*} not contain any attribute called *YT*. Then the tuple wrapping *t* WRAP ({*Y*} AS *YT*) is another tuple *s*. The heading of *s* consists of {*X*} extended with an attribute *YT* of type TUPLE {*Y*}. Let tuple *t* have *X* value *x*, *Y1* value *y1, Y2* value *y2, …,* and *Yn* value *yn*; then tuple *s* has *X* value *x* and *YT* value a tuple with *Y1* value *y1, Y2* value *y2, …,* and *Yn* value *yn*.

Example: Let *t* be the tuple for supplier S1 and part P1 from relvar SP. Then the expression

```
t WRAP ( { P#, QTY } AS PQ_TUP )
```

yields a tuple *tw* of type TUPLE {S# S#, PQ_TUP TUPLE {P# P#, QTY QTY}}, with S# value S1 and PQ_TUP value a tuple with P# value P1 and QTY value 300.

tuplevar A tuple variable.

two-valued logic Conventional logic, abbreviated 2VL, in which there are just two truth values, TRUE and FALSE.

type A named, finite set of values (not to be confused with the internal representation of the values in question, which is an implementation issue). Types can be either scalar or nonscalar (in particular, they can be tuple or relation types); consequently, attributes of relations can also be either scalar or nonscalar. Types can also be either system-defined (i.e., built-in) or user-defined. They can also be generated (*see* **type generator**). *Note:* A type isn't a value, nor is it a variable; in particular, relation values and relation variables aren't types. Equating types and either relation values or relation variables—a position that has been advocated in the literature—has been described as **The First Great Blunder**. (For the second, *see* **pointer**.)

Example: Here's a sample type definition:

```
TYPE POINT ...
    { ... CONSTRAINT ( X ** 2 + Y ** 2 ) ≤ 10000 } ;
```

POINT here is a user-defined type, denoting geometric points in two-dimensional space. It's subject to a type constraint that says, in effect, that the only points of interest are those that lie on or inside a circle with center the origin and radius 100.

Note: The (necessary) definition of the representation of POINT values in terms of the cartesian coordinates X and Y is deliberately omitted from the example, because a detailed discussion of that definition would take us too far afield. Other irrelevant details are also omitted for similar reasons.

type constraint A definition of the set of values that make up a given type. The type constraint for type *T* is checked when some selector is invoked for that type *T*; in other words, a type constraint error occurs if and only if some selector is invoked with arguments that violate the applicable type constraint. *Contrast* **type error**.

Example: See the POINT example under **type**.

type error The error that occurs if some operator is invoked with an argument that's not of the type of the corresponding parameter. Unlike integrity violations, such errors should be detectable at compile time (unless type inheritance is supported, in which case certain type errors—not all, by any means—might not be detectable until runtime).

type generator An operator that's invoked at compile time instead of run time and returns a type instead of a value. For example, conventional programming languages typically support an array type generator, which lets users define a variety of specific array types. In the relational model, the tuple and (especially) relation type generators are the most important ones; they allow users to define a variety of specific tuple and relation types. *See* **relation type**; **tuple type**.

Example: Consider the suppliers relvar definition:

```
VAR S BASE RELATION
  { S# S#, SNAME NAME, STATUS INTEGER, CITY CHAR }
    KEY { S# } ;
```

This definition includes an invocation of the RELATION type generator (syntactically, everything from the keyword RELATION to the closing brace following the keyword CHAR, inclusive). That invocation returns a specific relation type—viz., the type

```
RELATION
  { S# S#, SNAME NAME, STATUS INTEGER, CITY CHAR }
```

So this type is in fact a generated type—as indeed are all relation types, and all tuple types as well.

type inheritance An organizing principle according to which one type can be defined as a subtype of one or more other types, called supertypes (of the type in question). If $T2$ is a subtype of supertype $T1$, then all values of type $T2$ are also of type $T1$, and read-only operators and type constraints that apply to values of type $T1$ are inherited by values of type $T2$. However, values of type $T2$ will have read-only operators and type constraints of their own that don't apply to values that are only of type $T1$ and not $T2$.

unary Of degree one.

UNGROUP *See* ungrouping.

ungrouping Let s be a relation with an attribute YR of type RELATION $\{Y\}$, and let $\{X\}$ be the set of all attributes of s except YR. Let $\{Y\}$ have attributes $Y1, Y2, ..., Yn$; also, let $\{X\}$ not contain any attribute with the same name as any of $Y1, Y2, ..., Yn$. Then the ungrouping s UNGROUP (YR) is another relation r. The heading of r consists of the set theory union of $\{X\}$ and $\{Y\}$. As for the body, let z be a relation with heading consisting of $\{X\}$ extended with an attribute YT, of type TUPLE $\{Y\}$, and body defined as follows: for each tuple of s, z contains a set of tuples, one (t, say) for each tuple in the YR value in that s tuple; each such tuple t contains an X value (x, say) equal to the X value from the s tuple in question and a tuple value (yt, say) equal to some tuple from the YR value in the s tuple in question. Let z contain no other tuples. Then r is the result of z UNWRAP (YT).

Example: Let *spq* be the relation resulting from the expression

```
SP GROUP ( { P#, QTY } AS PQ_REL )
```

(*see* **grouping**). Then the expression

```
spq UNGROUP ( PQ_REL )
```

denotes an ungrouping of *spq*. That ungrouping is a relation of type RELATION {S# S#, P# P#, QTY QTY}, and if *spq* is obtained from the relation *sp* that is shown as the value of relvar SP in Figure 1, then the result of ungrouping *spq* is just *sp*. Suppose, however, that *spq* additionally includes a tuple, say for supplier S5, in which the PQ_REL value is an empty relation; the result of the foregoing UNGROUP won't contain a tuple for supplier S5 (in fact, the result will still be, exactly, relation *sp*). In general, therefore, ungrouping a relation *r* and then grouping it again in what might look like an inverse way isn't guaranteed to take us back to *r* (*contrast* **grouping**).

UNION *See* union.

union 1. *(Dyadic case)* The union of two relations *r1* and *r2*, *r1* UNION *r2*, where *r1* and *r2* are of the same type *T*, is a relation of type *T* with body the set of all tuples *t* such that *t* appears in either or both of *r1* and *r2*. 2. *(N-adic case)* The union of *n* relations *r1, r2, ..., rn* (*n* ≥ 0), UNION {*r1,r2,...,rn*}, where *r1, r2, ..., rn* are all of the same type *T*, is a relation of type *T* with body the set of all tuples *t* such that *t* appears in at least one of *r1, r2, ..., rn*. *Note:* If *n* = 0, (a) some syntactic mechanism, not shown here, is needed to specify the pertinent type *T*, and (b) the result is the empty relation of that type. *See also* **disjoint union**; **tuple union**.

Example: The expression (S{CITY}) UNION (P{CITY}) denotes the union of the projections on CITY of the relations that are the current values of relvars S and P. That union is a relation of type RELATION {CITY CHAR}. Moreover, if the current values of relvars S and P are *s* and *p*, respectively, the body of that relation consists of all tuples of the form <*c*> that appear in *s*{CITY} or *p*{CITY}, or both—meaning that *c* is a current supplier city or a current part city, or both.

union compatibility *(Of relations)* Of the same type. The term is deprecated for many reasons, of which inappropriateness is one.

union (set theory) The set of all elements appearing in either or both of two given sets. (This definition can obviously be extended to apply to any number of sets.)

unique index An implementation construct; not to be confused with a candidate key, q.v., even though such an index might be used to implement some key constraint (i.e., to enforce uniqueness of some candidate key).

universal quantifier Let *p*(*x*) be a predicate with a parameter *x*; then FORALL *x* (*p*(*x*)) is a predicate, and it means "For all argument values *v* that can replace the parameter *x*, *p*(*v*) is true." In this example, FORALL x is a universal quantifier, and x is a universally quantified bound variable (q.v.). *Note:* Some writers refer to FORALL by itself as the quantifier; the literature is not consistent on this point. More important, note that if $v1$, $v2$, ..., vn are all of the possible argument values in the foregoing example, then FORALL x $(p(x))$ is equivalent to $(p(v1))$ AND $(p(v2))$ AND ... AND $(p(vn))$ AND TRUE. Note in particular that this expression evaluates to TRUE if $n = 0$ (i.e., if the bound variable x ranges over an empty set).

Example: Here's a tuple calculus query that makes use of the universal quantifier as well as the existential quantifier ("Get suppliers who supply all parts"):

```
SX  RANGES OVER { S } ;
SPX RANGES OVER { SP } ;
PX  RANGES OVER { P } ;

SX WHERE
    FORALL PX ( EXISTS SPX ( SPX.S# = SX.S# AND
                             SPX.P# = PX.P# ) )
```

This latter expression can be read as "Suppliers SX where, for all parts PX, there exists a shipment SPX with the same supplier number as SX and the same part number as PX."

universal relation   Given a relation type RELATION $\{H\}$, the relation of that type that contains all possible tuples of type TUPLE $\{H\}$.

universal relvar   The join of all relvars in a given set of relvars. The normalization procedure of nonloss decomposition, if viewed in isolation (i.e., ignoring other possible aids to database design), tacitly assumes that it's possible to define an initial universal relvar that has all of the attributes relevant to the database under consideration, and then shows how that relvar can be replaced by successively "smaller" projections until a "good" design is reached. For a variety of reasons, however, that assumption is not very realistic.

UNWRAP   *See* unwrapping.

unwrapping   Let s be a relation with an attribute YT of type TUPLE $\{Y\}$, and $\{X\}$ be the set of all attributes of s except YT. Let $\{Y\}$ have attributes Y1, Y2, ..., Yn; also, let $\{X\}$ not contain any attribute with the same name as any of *Y1, Y2, ..., Yn*. Then the unwrapping *s* UNWRAP (*YT*) is another relation *r*. The heading of *r* consists of the set theory union of {*X*} and {*Y*}. The body of *r* contains one tuple for each tuple in *s*, and no other tuples. Let tuple *t* of *s* have *X* value *x* and *YT* value a tuple with *Y1* value *y1, Y2* value *y2, ..., and Yn* value *yn*; then the corresponding tuple of *r* has *X* value *x, Y1* value *y1, Y2* value *y2, ..., and Yn* value *yn*. See also **tuple unwrapping**.

Example: Let *spw* be the relation resulting from the expression

```
SP WRAP ( { P#, QTY } AS PQ_REL )
```

(*see* **wrapping**). Then the following expression denotes an unwrapping of *spw*:

```
spw UNWRAP ( PQ_REL )
```

That unwrapping is a relation of type RELATION {S# S#, P# P#, QTY QTY}. If *spw* is obtained by wrapping the relation *sp* that is shown as the value of relvar SP in Figure 1, then the result of unwrapping *spw* is just *sp*.

UPDATE 1. *(Read-only operator) See* **what if**. 2. *(Update operator)* Very loosely, an operator that modifies a given set of attributes in a given set of tuples in a given relvar; somewhat less loosely, an operator that replaces a given set of tuples in a given relvar by another such set. It's shorthand for a certain relational assignment.

Example (second definition only): The UPDATE statement

```
UPDATE P WHERE CITY = 'London'
     ( WEIGHT := 2 * WEIGHT , CITY := 'Oslo' ) ;
```

is shorthand for the following relational assignment:

```
P := WITH ( P WHERE CITY = 'London' ) AS t1 ,
          ( EXTEND t1 ADD
               ( 2 * WEIGHT AS NW ) ) AS t2 ,
          ( EXTEND t2 ADD
               ( 'Oslo' AS NC ) ) AS t3 ,
          ( t3 { P#, PNAME, COLOR, NW, NC } ) AS t4 ,
          ( t4 RENAME ( NW AS WEIGHT ) ) AS t5 ,
          ( t5 RENAME ( NC AS CITY ) AS t6 ,
          ( P MINUS t1 ) AS t7 :
       t7 UNION t6 ;
```

In this example, we might say, loosely, that attributes WEIGHT and CITY are being modified in the tuples for London parts; we might also say, still loosely but a little less so, that the tuples for London parts are being replaced; but what is really happening is that a certain relation value is being assigned to a certain relation variable.

UPDATE rule A specific kind of foreign key rule, q.v.

update A relational assignment (especially an INSERT, DELETE, or UPDATE operation).

update anomaly A somewhat old-fashioned term, never very precisely defined, for the kind of thing that can go wrong in a less than fully normalized database.

update operator An operator that, when invoked, returns no value but updates at least one variable (usually an argument) that's not local to the implementation of the operator in question. An update operator invocation thus has no value—it's not an expression, and it can't appear wherever an expression is required. In particular, it can't be nested inside expressions. Every update operator invocation is semantically equivalent to some assignment (possibly a multiple assignment, q.v.).

update propagation *See* controlled redundancy.

user Either an end user or an application programmer or both, as the context demands.

value An "individual constant," such as the integer value 3. Values can be of arbitrary complexity (they can be scalar or nonscalar; note in particular that tuples and relations are both values). Values have no location in time or space; however, they can be represented in memory by means of some encoding, and those representations do have locations in time and space—indeed, distinct representations of the same value can appear at any number of distinct locations in time and space, meaning, loosely, that the same value can appear as the current value of any number of distinct variables, and/or as any number of attribute values within the current value of any number of distinct tuplevars or relvars, at the same time or different times. Note that, by definition, a value can't be updated; for if it could, then after such an update it would no longer be that value. Note too that every value is of some type (in fact, of exactly one type, except possibly if type inheritance is supported). Note further that a value isn't a type, nor is it a variable. *Contrast* appearance.

VAR The **Tutorial D** operator for defining variables (relation variables in particular).

variable 1. *(Logic)* See logic variable. 2. *(Programming languages)* A holder for a representation of a value. Unlike values, variables (a) do have location in time and space and (b) can be updated (that is, the current value of the variable can be replaced by another value). Indeed, to be a variable is to be updatable; equivalently, to be a variable is to be assignable to (and to be assignable to is to be a variable). Note that every variable is declared to be of some type. Note further that a variable isn't a type, nor is it a value.

variable reference 1. *(Logic)* See bound variable; free variable. 2. *(Programming languages)* Syntactically, a variable name, used to denote either the variable as such or the value of that variable, as the context demands. Note in particular that such a reference certainly denotes the variable as such if it's used to specify a target for some update operation—in particular, if it appears on the left-hand side of an assignment. If on the other hand it denotes the value of the variable, then it's a special case of an expression, and it can appear wherever a literal (of the appropriate type) can appear.

view A derived relvar that's virtual, not real (*contrast* snapshot). The value of a given view at a given time is the result of evaluating a certain relational expression (the view-defining expression, specified when the view per se is defined) at the time in question. *Note:* The view-defining expression must mention at least one relvar, for otherwise the view wouldn't be, specifically, a relation variable. Note too that the view must be updatable for the same reason.

Example: The following statement defines a view called LSV:

```
VAR LSV VIRTUAL ( S WHERE CITY = 'London' ) ;
```

The relation that's the current value of view LSV at any given time is equal to the value of the view-defining expression S WHERE CITY = 'London' at that time.

view updating Either the theory or the process of updating views, as the context demands. View updating is still a somewhat controversial topic, but there are those who believe that—contrary to popular opinion—all views are at least theoretically updatable. The details are beyond the scope of this dictionary.

virtual relvar A view (*contrast* real relvar).

well-formed formula In logic, a formal expression denoting a predicate.

what if A read-only relational operator that returns the relation that would result if a given update were performed on a given relvar (at the time of invocation), without actually performing that update.

Example: Consider the following expression:

```
UPDATE S WHERE CITY = 'Paris'
    ( STATUS := 2 * STATUS , CITY := 'Nice' )
```

Observe that, even though it uses the keyword UPDATE, this expression is indeed an expression and not a statement (it has no terminating semicolon), and it has no effect on relvar S. What it does do is return a relation containing exactly one tuple *t* for each tuple *s* in relvar S for which the city is Paris—except that, in that tuple *t*, the status is double that in tuple *s* and the city is Nice, not Paris.

WITH A **Tutorial D** syntactic construct for introducing names for the results of subexpressions. The introduced names can then be used subsequently (within the overall expression of which the WITH clause forms a part) to denote those results.

Example: The following is a formulation of the query "Get pairs of supplier numbers, S*x* and S*y* say, such that S*x* and S*y* each supply exactly the same set of parts":

```
WITH ( S RENAME ( S# AS SX ) ) { SX } AS tx ,
     ( S RENAME ( S# AS SY ) ) { SY } AS ty :
( tx JOIN ty ) WHERE ( SP WHERE S# = SX ) { P# } =
                     ( SP WHERE S# = SY ) { P# }
```

WFF A well-formed formula. The abbreviation is variously pronounced "weff," "wiff," or "woof." *See also* closed WFF; open WFF.

WRAP *See* wrapping.

wrapping Let *r* be a relation and let the heading of *r* be partitioned into subsets {*X*} and {*Y*}. Let the attributes of {*Y*} be *Y1*, *Y2*, ..., *Yn*; also, let {*X*} not contain any attribute called *YT*. Then the wrapping *r* WRAP ({*Y*} AS *YT*) is another relation *s*. The heading of *s* consists of {*X*} extended with an attribute *YT* of type TUPLE {*Y*}. The body of *s* contains one tuple for each tuple in *r*, and no other tuples. Let tuple *t* of *r* have *X* value *x*, *Y1* value *y1*, *Y2* value *y2*, ..., and *Yn* value *yn*; then the corresponding tuple of *s* has *X* value *x* and *YT* value a tuple with *Y1* value *y1*, *Y2* value *y2*, ..., and *Yn* value *yn*. *See also* tuple wrapping.

Example: The following expression denotes a wrapping of the relation that's the current value of relvar SP:

```
SP WRAP ( { P#, QTY } AS PQ_TUP )
```

That wrapping is a relation *spw* of type RELATION {S# S#, PQ_TUP TUPLE {P# P#, QTY QTY}}; it contains one tuple for each tuple currently appearing in relvar SP, and no other tuples. Given the sample values in Figure 1, for example, the *spw* tuple for supplier S1 and part P1 has S# value S1 and a PQ_TUP value that is a tuple with P# value P1 and QTY value 300.

XML Extensible Markup Language; from a database point of view, best regarded as "just another data type" (albeit one of considerable pragmatic importance at the time of writing)—meaning, among other things, that relations should be allowed to have attributes of the type in question, and tuples in such relations should thus be allowed to include attribute values that are XML documents.

XOR *See* exclusive OR.

Related Titles from O'Reilly

Database

O'REILLY®

Our books are available at most retail and online bookstores.

To order direct: 1-800-998-9938 • *order@oreilly.com* • *www.oreilly.com*

Online editions of most O'Reilly titles are available by subscription at *safari.oreilly.com*